P9-CNC-515

FOOD NETWORK
SOUTH BEACH
WINE & FOOD
FESTIVAL COOKBOOK

FOOD NETWORK
SOUTH BEACH
WINE & FOOD
FESTIVAL COOKBOOK

Recipes and Behind-the-Scenes Stories from America's Hottest Chefs

Lee Brian Schrager with Julie Mautner
Foreword by Anthony Bourdain

Clarkson Potter/Publishers
New York

Proceeds from the *Food Network South Beach Wine & Food Festival Cookbook* will benefit the Florida International University School of Hospitality and Tourism Management and the Southern Wines & Spirits Beverage Management Center.

Published in the United States by Clarkson Potter/Publishers, an imprint of the Crown Publishing Group, a division of Random House, Inc., New York.
www.crownpublishing.com
www.clarksonpotter.com

CLARKSON POTTER is a trademark and POTTER with colophon is a registered trademark of Random House, Inc.

Library of Congress Cataloging-in-Publication Data
Schrager, Lee.
    The Food Network South Beach Wine & Food Festival cookbook / Lee Schrager. — 1st ed.
      p.   cm.
    Includes index.
    1. Cookery, American.   2. Festivals—Florida—Miami Beach. 3. South Beach
Wine and Food Festival (Miami Beach, Fla.)   I. South Beach Wine and Food
Festival (Miami Beach, Fla.)   II. Title.
    TX715.S14536   2011
    641.59759'381—dc22   2009052534

ISBN 978-0-307-46016-5

Printed in China

Design by Subtitle
Event photographs courtesy of Food Network South Beach Wine & Food Festival, except for page 6 (top left), page 7 (left, third from bottom), page 17, page 176 (center), and page 247 (bottom), which are copyright © 2010 by Quentin Bacon.

10   9   8   7   6   5   4   3   2   1

First Edition

CONTENTS

FOREWORD

BY ANTHONY BOURDAIN

Every year for the past five years, near the end of February, when the weather in New York is miserable and cold and I've been working too hard and away from friends too long, an escape is offered. I load a bathing suit, my loudest Hawaiian shirt, my most deteriorated jeans, and a pair of sandals into a suitcase and fly to Miami for the South Beach Wine & Food Festival.

I was never really a Miami fan. I was immune to the charms of *Miami Vice,* wondering always how many times a day Sonny Crockett had to change his white jacket. But for a few days each year, I step into a delicious alternate universe, a South Beach filled with wonderful things to eat, bags full of free stuff, and long afternoons at the pool accompanied by frosty boat drinks. And all my friends are there.

I got my first "swag bag" at the Festival—a benchmark moment in my career—entering my ludicrously large room at the Raleigh to find a sky-high tower of merch: professional-quality pots and pans, vanadium steel knives, every variety of appliance, a beach towel, liquors of many lands, and bottles of enticing mystery liquids ranging from energy water to exfoliant. I still have that lovely free beach towel—and my pores are cleaner than ever.

Ah, the many adventures. The festival seems to invite moments—and hours—of forgetfulness. Certainly it is advisable from a legal point of view to claim amnesia. Thinking back over the years, it's a tumble of images: padding onto the stage on the beach, sunburned and barefoot, fresh from the surf. Was that last year . . . or the year before . . . or is it every year? A hooting mob of industry types on Fridays, a more general audience on Saturdays. I remember screening the film I narrated, *Decoding Ferran Adrià,* for . . . Ferran Adrià (among the most terrifying and ultimately gratifying moments in my life) and, later, scooping the last Iranian beluga in the country into my face.

Then, at the delightfully divey Mac's Club at four in the morning, I remember seeing Nancy Silverton across the bar, still going strong. Nigella Lawson, barefoot and legs tucked under her on a couch, offering me cheese and charcuterie—and cigarettes. Thomas Keller smiling mischievously at me

and my soon wife-to-be from across a crowded dance floor. Elena Arzak plating food for the meal honoring Eric Ripert. Eric the next day, doing the breaststroke across the Raleigh pool, careful not to get his hair wet. Gabrielle Hamilton on her first trip to the festival, peeking around suspiciously and wondering—as I once did—what the hell she was doing here. The inexplicably energetic Iron Man of many continents, Daniel Boulud (one of the few chefs who needs only one name), dancing, a drink in his hand, somehow everywhere at once. Michael Ruhlman, sitting with me over drinks, about to get himself blackballed from television by agreeing to present our libelous "Golden Clog Awards"— a ludicrously faux award presentation ceremony in which we honored luminaries of the food world with hastily painted kitchen clogs, in categories like "Worst Career Move" and "Greatest Achievement in Hooves, Guts or Snouts," with one presenter after another

mysteriously vaporizing at the last minute. Rocco DiSpirito generously and good-naturedly agreed to present his namesake "Rocco Award" for "Worst Career Move." (The recipient showed no such good humor.)

The memory I have of Emeril—and one that, in many ways, sums up his true nature—is that every year, after the ceremonies, and after the parties, when a carload of drunken chefs on the spur of the moment decide to "swing by Emeril's," he is *always* to be found in the kitchen. An almost empty dining room, the last of the lingering dinner crowd, a boisterous incursion of colleagues at short notice—and there is Emeril, hunched over an outgoing order, looking up with a smile and greetings, happier in this element, a real, professional kitchen, than you've ever seen him on TV.

And, of course, I remember one particular carload of badly behaved chefs—an incongruous assemblage, to be sure: me, Mario Batali, Jamie Oliver, Mark Ladner,

BELOW: (From left to right) Honoring Emeril Lagasse at his Tribute Dinner in 2009. Paula Deen and Katie Lee.

Adam Perry Lang—crammed into the backseat of Lee Schrager's car, Lee chatting urgently but patiently over the phone, accommodating some last-minute diva, dealing with one of a thousand chef-related disasters large and small that he will face this weekend. Arranging for the disposal of a body, perhaps. We're on our way to a rooftop cocktail party? The Club Deuce? The Versace Mansion? To play capture the flag on the beach? To Emeril's to smoke cigars on the terrace and gossip about our peers and our betters? I don't remember. It could have been any or all of them.

None of this, neither madness nor glory, could have happened without Lee Schrager, who put the whole circus together, starting out in 2002 with 7,000 attendees and a dream. With astonishing speed he turned it into the combination Woodstock, Sundance, Cannes, and Altamont of the food world, the world's premier gathering of chefs— both spectacle (for ever larger audiences)

and refuge (for the chefs). For these few days in February, many of the greatest chefs in the world will meet like Mafia dons and relax. They will gossip, they will eat, they will party, they will reacquaint with old friends, they will receive news of far-flung associates and developments near and far—and, oh yeah, they will cook. While Rachael and Sandra and Guy and all the familiar Food Network faces have become more prominently represented, the professional dimension—the beating heart— remains strong.

For this alone, Lee Schrager is to be celebrated.

In this book there are recipes, photographs, and what I hope are severely edited stories from the past decade of the South Beach Wine & Food Festival. Schrager knows far more than he's telling. Too much.

I hope you enjoy reading and cooking as much as we enjoy remembering.

INTRODUCTION
RECIPE FOR SUCCESS

As a fortieth birthday gift, my friends Steven and Barbara Raichlen invited me to join them at the Aspen Food & Wine Classic. I walked into the tasting area, saw those beautiful mountains in the background, and knew instantly: a festival like this would be *amazing* on the beach.

That was 1999. Today the South Beach Wine & Food Festival is one of the largest and most successful food-and-wine events in the country. In ten years we've raised roughly $10 million for culinary and wine education at Florida International University and the Southern Wine & Spirits Beverage Management Center, allowed thousands of students to have hands-on experience, hosted hundreds of thousands of foodies and wine lovers, and showcased the best chefs in the world. This year, 50,000 people will attend at least one of our fifty festival events.

For one long weekend each February, the world's most popular chefs drop what they're doing to transform South Beach into the world's largest and liveliest kitchen, providing four days of nonstop food-and-wine-drenched decadence to those lucky enough to land a ticket.

While chefs and winemakers love the once-a-year chance to strut their stuff and to catch up with industry friends, festivalgoers love how SoBe allows them to mingle with insiders in a fabulous, informal setting.

"It's the sexiest food and wine event of the year," says restaurateur Drew Nieporent.

It's still hard for me to believe that a little wine and cheese tasting—I used to call it "my mother's fondue party on the beach"—somehow turned into *this* without any cohesive, long-term plan. The speed at which it happened caught us all by surprise. It was years, for example, before I realized I had better back up my trusty BlackBerry, which now contains 6,682 names.

The truth is, we're just a big bunch of passionate people, working hard for a great cause and having tons of fun. Over the years I've heard South Beach compared to the Cannes Film Festival and the Super Bowl; we've been called "the Sundance of the food and wine industry" and "the biggest beach party on the planet." In the *New York Times,* Frank Bruni declared SoBe "an exuberant Foodstock."

BACK IN THE DAY

I have wonderful early memories of food. My mother, Marlene, is a great cook who loved to make hearty dishes like Salisbury steak, braised lamb ribs, and an egg dish we called German Breakfast. For Mom, the Holy Trinity was Mimi Sheraton, Julia Child, and *The Joy of Cooking.*

My father, Ken, my brothers, Richard and Howard, and I were all passionate but picky eaters. On birthdays, everyone was allowed to pick his or her favorite restaurant—but the chance to get out of the kitchen for the night must have been a great

gift to Mom as well. To this day, I associate good food with good times.

When my parents went on vacation, they left my brothers and me with Mrs. C, an Italian grandma type who loved to cook and bake. I remember standing on a chair, making bread, pizza, and pasta with her. Anytime I walk into a bakery today, I think of Mrs. C.

I was the proud owner of both an Easy-Bake Oven and a Big Burger Grill. So while the other kids in Massapequa were clamming in Long Island Sound, my best friend, Steven Salinaro, and I were making little cakes and pizzas and selling them door-to-door. I had a stand in the yard where I sold hamburgers, too. I started cooking for real at age seven or eight, making patty melts and a huge mess.

So of course I went to the Culinary Institute of America, graduating in 1979.

But I never wanted to actually be a chef—I just wanted to know that I could. I knew I'd work in food and beverage, but beyond that I had no plan. I ended up in Miami, opening nightclubs, dabbling in gourmet retail, doing event planning, and working in various hotel jobs. I owned a health food restaurant for a while, and a dinner club with actor Mickey Rourke. Then I was hired by Southern Wine & Spirits in 2000 to be their director of media and special events. It was a fancy title at the country's largest distributor of alcoholic beverages. There was no job description and I hadn't a clue what I was supposed to do.

GET THIS PARTY STARTED

Luckily, Southern assigned me the task of upgrading a one-day wine tasting, called the Florida Extravaganza, that they had created to benefit Florida International University's School of Hospitality and Tourism Management. Held on the FIU campus in North

ABOVE: There's never an empty seat when Paula Deen takes the stage.

Miami, the event attracted 600 people and raised $30,000. I took one look and knew it had huge potential. And with images of Aspen dancing in my head, I decided to pick it up and plop it onto the most beautiful beach in the world.

To get the ball rolling and create a buzz, I knew I needed a "name." And what better name than Alain Ducasse to send the message that the South Beach Wine & Food Festival was going to get serious about food?

For help, I turned to my dear friend Terry Zarikian, the head of a Miami-based public relations firm specializing in chefs and restaurants. Terry agreed to help—and has played a huge role in the festival ever since.

"Lee nudged me to get Ducasse," Terry remembers. "I nudged restaurateur Jeffrey Chodorow. Jeffrey nudged Alain Ducasse and Alain said yes. That sort of made the festival for us . . . and the rest is history."

Nobu Matsuhisa, Garry Danko, Cindy Pawlcyn, François Payard, Todd English,

Drew Nieporent, Mark Militello, Allen Susser, and Norman Van Aken also signed on that first year, which sweetened the pot further still. Seven thousand people came.

Ducasse agreed to come back the second year, and Bobby Flay came aboard too. So did Alice Waters, Michael Mina, Rocco DiSpirito, Hubert Keller, Alfred Portale, Pierre Hermé, Daniel Boulud, and Eric Ripert.

Then *Food & Wine* signed on as our presenting sponsor, which was almost too good to be true. Not only did they pay a hefty sponsorship fee, but their name also gave us instant credibility with both chefs and consumers.

I had started nudging Food Network to sponsor us way back in 2003, but Brooke Johnson, the president, said, "All my chefs are there anyway. Why do I have to give you money?" Then I ran into her on the subway in New York and discovered we have apartments in the same Upper West Side building.

ABOVE: Toasting Daniel Boulud at his Tribute Dinner in 2010.

Our friendship grew from there. Brooke came to the festival and saw what we were doing. On her way home, she sent me an e-mail that said, "Lee, I get it now."

In 2007, Food Network came aboard as Title Sponsor, bringing with them their incredible marketing machine. The Food Network name gave us cachet and also colossal media play. Our partnership with them really took us to the next level.

"The festival is hugely successful, and we're thrilled to be a part of it," Brooke says today.

I think few would argue that SoBe long ago eclipsed all other events of its type in terms of A-list attendance, industry relevance, food and wine quality, and fun factor. "Anyone who's important is there, having the time of their life," says Wolfgang Puck.

"It's just wonderful to remember where the festival began and to see how it's grown," says Mel Dick, partner and president of the wine division at Southern Wine & Spirits.

"It gives me enormous pleasure to know that our company is behind it."

Over the years the Festival has also become a forum for important industry issues, and the concept of wellness is a theme that subtly pervades many of our events.

In 2008, for example, a luncheon panel discussion focused on childhood obesity; it was a complete sellout and has been re-invented each year. Our Kidz Kitchen program, featuring hands-on cooking lessons with celebrity chefs, has morphed into its own "festival within a festival" called Fun and Fit as a Family, sponsored by South Beach Diet at Miami's Jungle Island. The money it raises stays in the community to support local charities.

People have this impression that the chefs all come down here to party—Emeril calls SoBe "Spring Break for Chefs"—but the truth is they probably work harder here than they do at home. However, they rarely turn us down when we invite them to come and cook. "It's like a family reunion," says Tyler Florence. "The organization is impeccable and there are star chefs *everywhere*. You guys raise the bar every year."

LAY OF THE SAND

The festival events start Thursday evening with the Burger Bash. We try to concentrate the festivities as tightly as possible within an eight-block patch of beachfront paradise, but we also use the Biltmore, the Mandarin Oriental, the Fontainebleau, and other exceptional venues around town.

Home base is the 60,000-square-foot "Grand Tasting Village," sprawled across the sand between 10th and 13th streets. It's here that 200 or so companies (restaurants, wine and spirit suppliers, exhibitors, sponsors) serve up their chicken chicharones and mango mojitos and whatever else they feel like dishing up or pouring out for the 20,000 or so guests who'll pass through the tents on Saturday or Sunday. And it's here that thirty or so big-name chefs will do cooking demos for capacity crowds of up to 700 people each, with hundreds more milling around the edges.

Then there's the North Venue: two vast 100- by 300-foot tents on the beach behind the Delano and the Ritz-Carlton, where we hold the Burger Bash and the BubbleQ. Other restaurants, hotels, and clubs host

ABOVE: Cesare Casella at Best of the Best in 2010.

festival events or graciously give us their kitchens for prep.

But command central—the festival's heart—is the Loews Miami Beach. It's our HQ for the week and our home away from home. And they do a heroic job! Not only is the Loews kitchen an informal hospitality suite for all visiting chefs, it also handles production for much of the food served on the beach. The Loews also hosts the Saturday Night Tribute Dinner, a glittering gala where a group of superlative chefs comes in to cook for a chef we've chosen to honor and the 600 or so guests lucky enough to get a ticket before they sell out. When the brigade for one evening includes five or six of the top names in the business—people like Thomas Keller, Jean-Georges Vongerichten, Gray Kunz, Charlie Trotter, Ferran Adrià, Daniel Boulud, and Eric Ripert, to name a few— you know this is not your local Rotary Club dinner.

For the first six years of the festival, the Loews' exec chef was Marc Ehrler, and he remembers the pandemonium as huge fun. "We'd have some of the biggest egos in the industry in my kitchen, all working side by side," he recalls. "But everyone helps everyone, and that's what makes the festival so great. I used to get so excited before SoBe that for many nights I literally couldn't sleep."

In 2007, Marc left Miami to become corporate executive chef for Loews Hotels & Resorts, and he passed the torch to Gordon Maybury, who displayed the same "whatever whenever" attitude that we love.

"It's a big deal and a lot of pressure," Maybury says of the festival weekend and the meals his kitchen has turned out. "We're in awe of some of these guest chefs, but we want them to be in awe of us too. We want to showcase a flawless operation. The weekend consists of many moving parts and many egos in one kitchen. It makes me very very nervous but I wouldn't trade it for anything."

GRILLED FOR ONE MINUTE
BROOKE JOHNSON
PRESIDENT, FOOD NETWORK

Q: When I first approached you about sponsoring the festival, you turned me down. So what finally changed your mind? Was it that muffin basket I sent over?

A: Nope . . . you just kind of wormed your way into my affection, which I think is your MO! And I discovered that you're a great guy, and fun to be around. We became friends. I finally signed on as Title Sponsor in 2007.

Q: What do you love most about the festival, personally?

A: Hanging out with some of my favorite people, who happen to work at Food Network . . . all the major talent in one place. They're super fun to be around, especially in a no-pressure, everyone's-having-a-good-time situation. Also, seeing how the crowd reacts to our chefs. It's amazing!

Q: Every foodie we know wants to be on Food Network. You must hear it all the time: *I have a great idea for a show! Put me on the air!* How often, actually, are you pitched?

A: Hundreds and hundreds of times each year. Tons.

Q: Who gets a chance and who doesn't?

A: In general we look for an expertise, so be expert at what you're doing. And for passion and raw enthusiasm. We also look for something unique. And you should have experience cooking either on TV or in front of people. It looks super easy, but talking while cooking is surprisingly difficult.

Q: What's the best part of your job?

A: The people I work with. They're gregarious; they love to eat and drink. And as a businessperson I find it really refreshing that they see both sides of the equation: art and commerce. Plus, they're giving. People who choose food service in the first place tend to like giving. But the people we work with are involved, often enormously, in charity work. That's another part of what makes them so interesting to be around. I'm talking not just about our talent but also the whole Food Network family.

Q: And the worst part of your job?

A: This is the best job I've ever had and I feel very, very lucky.

Q: What do you eat when no one is watching?

A: I could live on bread, cheese, and wine. And I'm ashamed to admit I'm a bit of a candy person . . . so it would be Hershey bars that I eat when no one's looking.

Q: Would you like to be on TV?

A: No. I was on TV years ago. I started out as a local news reporter and got it out of my system!

MY MOST MEMORABLE SOBE MOMENTS

Getting Alain Ducasse here our first year, thanks to Jeffrey Chodorow.

Honoring the king and queen of Spain in 2009, and Mario Batali's drunken rantings at their Viva España dinner. He finally apologized.

Gordon Ramsay's mystery disappearance; to this day we don't know what happened.

The entire *Today Show* being taped at the festival in 2008.

Honoring Ferran Adrià in 2007 with Thomas Keller, Nobu Matsuhisa, Jean-Georges Vongerichten, José Andrés, and Pierre Hermé cooking the dinner.

The first BubbleQ, hosted by Steven Raichlen in 2002. It put us on the map.

Willie Nelson performing at the BubbleQ in 2004.

The monsoon that hit us in 2006, the year Bobby Flay hosted the BubbleQ.

Honoring Jamie Oliver with our Global Citizen Award in 2008 and Alice Waters presenting it.

Creating the Burger Bash with Rachael Ray and seeing it quickly become our most popular event.

The eighty-piece Miami Central High School Marching Band bursting into the Loews ballroom playing "When the Saints Go Marching In" at full volume, as a grand finale to the Tribute Dinner honoring Emeril in 2009.

Bringing together Peter and Robert Mondavi (above, left to right) to lead the tasting of the wines they made together after their many-year, much-publicized feud.

THE FUN IN FUND-RAISING

SoBe gets tons of press for our rock-star chefs, our late-night parties, and the crowds at the Burger Bash and the BubbleQ. What's far more important to me, however, is all the good we do. We draw national and international attention to Miami, its chefs, restaurants, hotels, and attractions. We generate big bucks for the local economy, from hotel rooms, restaurant meals, shopping, and such. We give wine lovers the chance to expand their knowledge and taste vintages they'll never find elsewhere.

But most important of all, SoBe raises serious money, now donating upwards of $2 million each year for wine, culinary, and hospitality education through FIU's School of Hospitality and Tourism Management and the Southern Wine & Spirits Beverage Management Center. In ten years we've given roughly 8,000 students the chance to rub white-jacketed shoulders with world-class chefs; many get internships and jobs thanks to their festival work. I bump into FIU grads all the time who tell me how our funding has helped launch or build their careers. The satisfaction that brings me is immeasurable. Many students return after graduation as festival volunteers.

SOBE IT!

First-timers at SoBe tend to be a bit shocked by the vastness of it all: the number of different events to choose from, the caliber of the chefs, the volume and quality of the wines, the attention paid to detail. It's an enormous undertaking that takes us a good eighteen months of planning to pull off.

At the five-year mark, we threw ourselves a party. Many of you were there. But our tenth anniversary seemed to warrant something richer and more lasting—hence this celebratory cookbook. We set out to capture festival moments, memories, and milestones—and to highlight some sensational dishes from a selection of SoBe chefs. We set out to create a family scrapbook, but our SoBe family is huge! We were able to include only a fraction of what we wanted to.

First we put out the call for recipes. I had imagined dishes that were feasible for home cooks with average skills, dishes that could be made in relatively little time from readily available ingredients in a typical foodie home kitchen.

Ha! Who was I kidding?

One chef sent a "simple" recipe calling for lobster stock, Dungeness crab, sea urchin roe, and gelatin sheets. Another recipe listed thirty-five different ingredients, plus "salt and pepper to taste."

Another chef sent a recipe that sounded so good, I almost jumped up right then and there to make it. Then I realized I'd need a Cryovac machine, an immersion circulator, a Parisienne (a scoop, not a person), 10 pounds of veal bones, 5 pounds of oxtail, 12 baby cucumbers in blossom, and 12 "mini air breads."

For the most part, however, our chefs got it . . . and they flooded us with fantastic choices. This led, of course, to the next problem: *way too many tempting dishes to choose from.* Thus began the formidable task of picking just the right mix; we wanted starters, main courses, and desserts; poultry, beef, pork, lamb, and seafood. We wanted dishes either prepared at SoBe or with a SoBe feel, and we definitely wanted to display the festival's vivid multicultural flavor. The juggling went on for months as we carefully pieced the puzzle together; some chefs patiently sent recipe after recipe until we found one we agreed was perfect.

And then we sent them all off to be tested, enlisting Michael and Elaina Moran for the task. Their test reports were coming back filled with rave reviews:

"An amazing dish with outstanding flavor and presentation!" the Morans wrote of Jean-Georges Vongerichten's lamb.

"Wow, love this dish!" they gushed about Alfred Portale's shrimp. "All hail chef Portale!"

Given SoBe's singular setting and the availability of pristine seafood, you'll see we've emphasized shellfish and fish. You'll also find lots of small plates, because so many SoBe dishes are served this way. You'll find a hearty selection of burgers and barbecue, drawn from our two most popular events, and terrific main courses too. Some of our recipes are more complex than others—we call those the "dare you" dishes—and others are simple enough for beginners. But we think all of them are exceptional.

Celebrating our tenth anniversary this year has given us an ideal opportunity to take stock. Our New York City Wine & Food Festival, founded in 2007, is now an undeniable hit, and other cities are to come. But SoBe will always hold a special place in my heart, and I know that everyone at Southern Wine & Spirits feels the same. So here's to ten more years of great times on the beach . . . I can't wait to see you there.

CHAPTER 1
DRINKS

OPPOSITE: (From left to right) Sandra Lee's drink demos are a festival favorite. Champagne flowing at SoBe.

In South Beach, for a couple of days each February, Champagne becomes one of the four basic food groups.

Scores of otherwise rational people enjoy elegant six-course meals, then head for a hotel rooftop lounge for sliders and vodka cocktails—stopping at a dessert party in between.

At SoBe, someone introducing himself as a "wine shepherd," a "master mixologist," a "swirler/sniffer," or an "ice artist" is probably not pulling your leg.

With Southern Wine & Spirits as its host, the festival sets the standard when it comes to all things wonderful to drink. Wine guru Josh Wesson calls SoBe "a grape-stained fun park, a sandy Disneyland of food and drink."

Since the first year of the fest, wine has played the starring role. But as cocktails have grown increasingly popular, they've become an important part of the mix. Today, the volume and range of beverages served at SoBe is both ridiculous and sublime: from agave nectar to Zinfandel, you can sip from a sea of choices. The products come from all over the world, and new ones are launched here every year. But whether it's a First-Growth Bordeaux for a formal dinner or an icy beer for a barbecue, event managers work all year long to ensure that only the best is served at the fest.

When it comes to pairing wine with meals, for example, the attention to detail is astounding. In 2005, Laurent-Perrier Champagne was concerned that the crisp sage glaze on Michel Roux's crusted veal chop would clash with their Grand Siècle Alexandra Rosé 1997. So Terry Zarikian, then the festival's culinary and PR director, rang the Michelin three-star chef in London to suggest swapping basil for sage.

"That worked for the dish and made the Champagne happy too," Zarikian remembers.

Speaking of Champagne, it flows here morning, noon, and night. By your second day at SoBe, you'll wonder how you ever lived a day without it.

22

But surrounding all this eating and drinking, there is a lot to be learned as well; we offer guided tastings and seminars for every skill level and interest. Over the years, thousands of SoBe guests have sipped with top sommeliers, mastered the making of the hottest new and classic cocktails, and found perfect pairings for Latin food, barbecue,

"Pinot Noir vs. Merlot." These small-group tastings are usually led by the winemaker or vineyard owner himself.

Another SoBe tradition is the themed late-night cocktail party with a celebrity foodie host. Elegant yet informal, these parties let guests schmooze with Bobby Flay, Paula Deen, Guy Fieri, Tyler Florence, Katie

chocolate, ceviche, sushi, and even hot dogs.

If you're curious about trends in food and drink, a day in our Grand Tasting Village will tell you all you need to know. This is where leading wineries pour new releases, bartenders transform tropical fruits into irresistible concoctions, and top South Florida chefs serve up tapas-size plates of their most popular restaurant dishes. A steel-drum band and cooking demos contribute to the beach-party atmosphere.

Meanwhile, down the road, there's an entirely different scene: serious comparative tastings of iconic wines, held for just fifty to a hundred people at a time. Opus One, Pétrus, Lafite Rothschild, Château Haut-Brion, and Screaming Eagle illustrate the caliber. Comparison tastings are also hot tickets: think "Barolo vs. Brunello" and

Lee, and others. And when an event is sponsored by Patrón, Ketel One, Belvedere, or Cîroc, for example, you know the cocktails are going to be fantastic.

"And then," says restaurant consultant Clark Wolf, "after the after *after* party . . . there's that brilliant sunrise over those magnificent beaches and another sun-drenched day filled with a universe of nibbles and sips."

No one eats or drinks this way in real life, of course. But for a couple of days each year, the festival allows people to gather for an important cause and devote themselves to pleasure.

SoBe has had a number of slogans over the years, but "moderation in moderation" says it best. So here are some of our favorite cocktail recipes to tide you over until next year!

TONY ABOU-GANIM
SUNSPLASH

I invented this colorful feel-good drink at Harry Denton's Starlight Room in San Francisco in 1996. It's a fruity cooler with "poolside" written all over it, perfect for a sunny afternoon with friends, which is why it was ideal at SoBe. Which vodka you use is a matter of taste: some have bursts of orange blossom and hints of lime; others bring in notes of marmalade and lemon.

SERVES 1

Ice cubes

1½ ounces orange vodka

1½ ounces freshly squeezed orange juice

1½ ounces cranberry juice

1 ounce Fresh Lemon Sour (recipe follows)

½ ounce orange liqueur

1 slice orange, for garnish

1 strip lemon peel, formed into a spiral, for garnish

In an ice-filled mixing glass, combine the vodka, juices, lemon sour, and liqueur. Shake vigorously. Pour through a cocktail strainer into an ice-filled tumbler. Garnish with the orange slice and lemon peel.

FRESH LEMON SOUR

Mix 2 parts strained freshly squeezed lemon juice with 1 part simple syrup (equal parts sugar and water boiled until the sugar has dissolved, then cooled).

DALE DEGROFF
HONEYSUCKLE ROSE

This cocktail was inevitable. I came up with it on the island of Mykonos while creating a menu for the beautiful Belvedere Hotel. The local thyme, honey, and mint were so intense that just putting them together in a bowl and being in the same room was intoxicating!

SERVES 1

2 sprigs fresh thyme

2 sprigs fresh mint

1 ounce freshly squeezed lemon juice

1½ ounces ouzo

⅔ ounce honey syrup (half honey and half water dissolved together)

1½ ounces water

Ice cubes

In a tall glass, muddle 1 sprig of the thyme and 1 sprig of the mint with the lemon juice. Add the ouzo, honey syrup, and water. Stir, and add some ice to the glass. Garnish with the remaining thyme and mint sprigs, and serve with a straw.

GRILLED FOR ONE MINUTE
FRANCIS FORD COPPOLA

FILMMAKER AND VINTNER

Q. Who was your winemaking or wine-business mentor?

A: I was introduced to fine wine by two people: Gore Vidal and, in odd circumstances, Bill Cosby. Bill didn't drink, but he always poured good wines for guests.

Q: In what ways is the wine world different today than when you were getting started?

A: Wine styles have certainly evolved. Over the years, wines have become higher in alcohol, fresher, and fruitier.

Q: How is the movie business similar to the wine business?

A: The process of making film and wine is very similar. There are three phases: the gathering of the source material, the production, and the finishing.

Q: What do you drink in your home theater, and does the wine change with the theme of the movie?

A: We rarely, if at all, eat or drink in the home theater.

Q: Do you have a favorite food or wine movie?

A: Ang Lee's *Eat Drink Man Woman* and Alexander Payne's *Sideways.*

ABOVE: Mel Dick of Southern Wine & Spirits presented Francis Ford Coppola with a Lifetime Achievement Award in 2005.

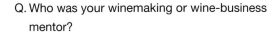

"THERE'S ONE OLDER COUPLE, PROBABLY IN THEIR SEVENTIES OR EIGHTIES, WHO'VE COME TO SOBE AT LEAST THREE YEARS IN A ROW (THAT I KNOW OF), TRYING TO CRASH AND CLAIMING TO HAVE BEEN INVITED BY VARIOUS PEOPLE, NONE OF THEM KNOWN TO US. SO FAR I'VE KICKED THEM OUT OF THE BURGER BASH, THE BEST OF THE BEST, THE TRIBUTE DINNER, AND THE OSCAR PARTY IN 2009. I LOOK FORWARD TO IT EVERY YEAR!"

—PATRICK JONG, MARKETING DIRECTOR, SBWFF

SANDRA LEE
LEMON-CUCUMBER COCKTAIL

When I throw a party, I like to greet my guests with a fabulous drink like this—it makes them feel welcome. My friends love this cocktail because it's fresh and light, which means it's perfect for a party on the beach or a gathering in the garden.

SERVES 12

3 10-ounce bottles club soda

1 cup gin

¼ cup bottled lemon juice

12 thin slices lemon

12 thin slices cucumber

12 cups crushed ice

12 sprigs fresh mint, for garnish (optional)

In a large pitcher, combine the club soda, gin, and lemon juice. Place a lemon slice and a cucumber slice in each of 12 glasses. Add 1 cup of the crushed ice to each glass. Pour the gin mixture into the glasses and garnish each with a mint sprig if desired.

LOEWS MIAMI BEACH HOTEL
CLASSIC MOJITO

Miami has amazing mojitos, and we're known for having one of the best. Our bartenders hand-muddle each and every mojito, giving them all extra-special love and care! Fresh local ingredients and great rum make this cocktail a winner—it's definitely a guest favorite.

SERVES 1

6 lime wedges

6 large fresh mint leaves

½ ounce simple syrup (equal parts sugar and water boiled until the sugar has dissolved, then cooled)

Ice cubes

3 ounces light rum

Club soda

Sugarcane stick, for garnish

In a cocktail mixing tin, muddle 5 of the lime wedges, the mint, and the syrup. Cover with ice and add the rum. Cover and shake. Pour the drink into a highball glass; top with a splash of club soda. Garnish with the remaining lime wedge and the sugarcane.

ALLEN KATZ
VERMILLION

Ranging in color from pink to vibrant sunset red, the Vermillion has a real South Beach feel.

SERVES 1

Crushed ice

1½ ounces gin

1½ ounces light rum

1½ ounces freshly squeezed lemon juice

½ ounce grenadine

1 strip grapefruit peel, formed into a spiral, for garnish

In an ice-filled cocktail shaker, combine the gin, rum, lemon juice, and grenadine. Shake vigorously. Pour through a cocktail strainer into a chilled cocktail glass. Garnish with the grapefruit peel, and serve.

SUSAN SPICER
SATSUMA MARGARITA WITH BASIL

When I first made this cocktail, it was a warm and sunny New Orleans winter day. So I think of it as a nice way to celebrate winter with warmth, color, and fresh flavor. The basil gives it a bit of a spicy bite.

SERVES 2

Ice cubes

1 cup freshly squeezed satsuma orange or tangerine juice (4 or 5 oranges)

6 ounces premium tequila

2 ounces orange liqueur

6 medium to large fresh basil or Thai basil leaves, torn, plus 2 sprigs, for garnish

1 tablespoon Triple Sec

In an ice-filled cocktail shaker, combine the juice, tequila, liqueur, and basil leaves. Shake vigorously. Pour, straining out the basil leaves, into 2 chilled margarita glasses straight up, or serve on the rocks if desired. Lace each drink with ½ tablespoon of the Triple Sec. Garnish each drink with a basil sprig, and serve.

" IN 2007, ROBERT AND PETER MONDAVI MADE A RARE JOINT APPEARANCE TO POUR TWO NAPA VALLEY CABERNETS THEY MADE TOGETHER, 1965 CHARLES KRUG AND 2004 ANCORA UNA VOLTA. THE WINES WERE IMPRESSIVE, AND THE EMOTIONAL IMPACT OF THE FAMILY REUNION BROUGHT A CAPACITY CROWD TO ITS FEET IN A PROLONGED STANDING OVATION FOR THE PROUD OLD MEN. "

—THOMAS MATTHEWS, EXECUTIVE EDITOR OF *WINE SPECTATOR,*
SOBE WINE SEMINAR LEADER, AND BEST OF THE BEST EVENT HOST

ANGELO VIEIRA
MIXED BERRY CAIPIRINHA

The caipirinha is Brazil's national cocktail, made with Brazil's noble and national spirit, cachaça. (Cachaça can be made only in Brazil, like tequila in Mexico and true Champagne in France.) This is my twisted version of the classic drink, made by adding fresh berries and liqueurs while maintaining the base of lime, cachaça, and sugar. It's refreshing, but its stealth characteristics still pack a punch, just like the original! This is one of our best sellers at Sunset Lounge in The Mondrian Miami, and it was a huge hit at SoBe as well.

SERVES 1

2 teaspoons muscovado or turbinado sugar	1½ ounces cachaça
1 lime, cut into 6 wedges	¼ ounce crème de framboise
3 fresh raspberries	¼ ounce crème de mûre
2 fresh blackberries	¼ ounce crème de fraise
2 fresh strawberries	1 scoop crushed or shaved ice

Place the sugar in a double old-fashioned glass. Squeeze the lime wedges over the sugar before dropping them into the glass. Add 2 raspberries, 1 blackberry, and 1 strawberry. Muddle, releasing all the oils from the lime skins and crushing the berries. Add the cachaça and the liqueurs. Stir, using a bar spoon, until the ingredients start to combine and the sugar starts to melt. Add ½ scoop of the crushed ice and stir until the glass is cold and most of the sugar has melted. Cap the entire cocktail with the remaining crushed ice. Cut the remaining strawberry in half. Garnish the ice cap with a strawberry half and the remaining raspberry and blackberry, and serve.

FRANCESCO LAFRANCONI
PIÑA PIRINHA

In the Piña Pirinha, the exotic tropical flavor of pineapple from the infused vodka mixes beautifully with the more rustic and mellow cachaça. And it all gets laced together with agave nectar and chunks of lime, muddled to extract the juices and essential oils. An irresistible combination!

SERVES 1

5 lime wedges, halved

¾ ounce agave nectar

1 ounce cachaça

1 ounce pineapple vodka

Ice cubes

In the bottom of a Boston shaker glass, muddle the lime wedges with the agave nectar. Add the cachaça, the vodka, and 1 cup of ice. Shake vigorously and pour everything into a double old-fashioned glass (without straining).

“NOW I GET WHAT ALL THE FUSS IS ABOUT: SOUTH BEACH IS SO CHIC AND THE ENERGY IS OFF THE CHARTS. IT'S SO GREAT TO PAL AROUND WITH INDUSTRY LEADERS WHO'VE BEEN FRIENDS OF MINE FOR YEARS . . . AND THE PARTIES ARE TREMENDOUS! I'LL BE BACK!”

—RICK MOONEN

JOHN GRAY
MANGO-YOGURT SMOOTHIE kid friendly

My kids, Jack and Daniela, really love this drink, and it's super-simple to make. It's particularly great in the morning when you wake up and it's already hot outside.

SERVES 4

4 cups ice cubes

1½ cups diced peeled fresh mango

1¼ cups plain yogurt

3 tablespoons honey

Juice of ½ lime

Combine the ice, mango, yogurt, honey, and lime juice in a blender and process until smooth. Pour into tall glasses, and serve.

INGRID HOFFMANN
FROZEN POPS

These grown-up Popsicles appeal to the inner child in all of us . . . they're *delicioso,* refreshing, and so playful. I love to bring them out on a tray, with a bucket of ice and the popsicles on top, and glasses filled with different spirits and garnishes such as rock salt, turbinado sugar, and shredded toasted coconut. Plus, you need pretty napkins.

FROZEN PIÑA COLADA POPS

SERVES 6

½ cup rum or pineapple juice

6 frozen coconut all-fruit popsicles

1 cup Demerara or turbinado sugar

Toasted coconut flakes

Pour the rum into a tall, narrow glass. Remove the frozen pops from their wrappers and submerge them, one by one, in the glass of rum, tilting the glass to completely moisten the entire popsicle. Then sprinkle each side of the frozen pops with some sugar. Arrange the pops on a plate, sprinkle with the coconut, and serve immediately.

FROZEN MARGARITA POPS

SERVES 6

½ cup tequila

6 frozen lime all-fruit popsicles

Margarita salt or kosher salt

Pour the tequila into a tall, narrow glass. Remove the frozen pops from their wrappers and submerge them, one by one, in the glass of tequila, tilting the glass to completely moisten the entire popsicle. Then sprinkle each side of the frozen pops with some salt. Arrange the pops on a plate, and serve immediately.

CHAPTER 2
STARTERS AND SMALL PLATES

When I eat out, I often order a few appetizers and skip the entrée. I love to have a few bites of something, then move on to something else. Call it CADD: Culinary Attention Deficit Disorder.

I see my friends doing the same thing. In fact, when I eat out with a group, we'll often order every app on the menu—plus one or two entrées for good measure—and share it all. There's something so festive about all those pretty little plates spread across the table. I love exotic ingredients, bold flavors, creative combinations. And I generally find that chefs and home cooks who play it safe with their main courses tend to take more risks—and have more fun—with their starters.

Running around Miami Beach trying to get to as many SoBe events as possible, I'm always thrilled to see how our food has such a marvelous multi-culti vibe. It's in the starters, I think, that that flavor comes through most clearly. Call them tapas, snacks, nibbles, mezze, hors d'oeuvres, first courses, starters, small plates, little bites, or finger foods . . . a weekend at SoBe offers scores of opportunities for amazing grazing.

The Best of the Best, one of our most popular events, is a huge dine-around where forty or so fantastic chefs serve up small portions of their favorite dishes in the ballroom of the Fontainebleau Hotel. The crowd numbers 1,500 to 2,000, and each chef prepares about 500 servings. When we invite the chefs to come and cook, we request that they themselves do the honors. So our guests get to sample myriad different dishes and chat with a slew of world-class chefs. Each dish is offered with wine rated 90 or higher by *Wine Spectator,* the party's sponsor, typically poured by the winemaker or the vineyard owner himself.

When I entertain at home, I love to serve up a whole mess of appetizers, pulling recipes from my favorite chefs' books. But whether I'm hosting an intimate evening for friends and family or a festival party for thousands, my goal remains the same: to provide warm and welcoming hospitality with ample food and drink. I want people to leave my parties at the end of the evening saying, "Wow!"

With fifty-some different events over the festival weekend—and a large selection of small plates served at most of them—you can imagine the difficulty we had in choosing the recipes for this chapter. I think this is a spectacular assortment that conveys the feel and the flavor of SoBe.

DAVID BOULEY
BIGEYE TUNA CARPACCIO WITH YUZU-MISO DRESSING AND HERBS

This dish was inspired by the Tsuji Cooking Academy in Osaka, Japan, where I have a long relationship as both student and teacher. The professors and I tested more than 800 recipes for the opening of one of my restaurants in New York . . . and this was one of our favorites. It's an easy dish to prepare but nutritionally complex, filled with minerals, calcium, zinc, probiotics, and protein.

SERVES 6

YUZU-MISO DRESSING

⅓ cup tomato water (from 3 beefsteak tomatoes; see step 1)

⅔ cup sweet white miso

1 tablespoon crème fraîche

1 teaspoon olive oil

1 tablespoon yuzu juice

Salt

Freshly ground white pepper

TUNA SEASONING BATH

⅓ cup sake

⅓ cup mirin

¼ cup soy sauce

1 teaspoon yuzu juice

1 small piece kombu seaweed

8 ounces sashimi-grade bigeye tuna

1 cup micro greens and/or herbs (celery, shervil, tarragon, radish, dill, basil)

FOR THE YUZU-MISO DRESSING

1. To make the tomato water, blend the tomatoes, seasoned with ¼ to ½ teaspoon salt, into a smooth purée. Place in a cheesecloth-lined strainer set over a bowl; let it strain overnight.

2. In a bowl, combine the miso, tomato water, crème fraîche, oil, and yuzu juice; whisk or blend until smooth and completely emulsified. Season with salt and pepper to taste, and let the dressing rest overnight in the refrigerator.

FOR THE TUNA SEASONING BATH

In another bowl, combine the sake, mirin, soy sauce, yuzu juice, and seaweed, and let the mixture rest overnight in the refrigerator.

TO SERVE

Thinly slice the tuna into wide square pieces—the thinner, the better. Then bathe it in the seasoning bath for 2 minutes. On each plate, spread the yuzu-miso dressing in a thin round. Take the tuna from the bath and let the liquid run off. Place the tuna slices over the dressing, and garnish with the micro greens.

THOMAS KELLER

WHITE STURGEON CAVIAR WITH "CRÊPE AU MOUSSE DE CRÈME FRAÎCHE," SNIPPED GARDEN CHIVES, AND MEYER LEMON SYRUP

I like this recipe because it's a riff on the classic pairing of blinis with caviar. The caviar conveys a sense of luxury, so it elevates any celebration—the same way a great bottle of Champagne would.

SERVES 12

CRÊPES	SYRUP
1¼ cups milk	½ cup water
3 large eggs	½ cup sugar
2 tablespoons butter, melted	¼ cup freshly squeezed Meyer lemon juice
½ cup all-purpose flour	
1½ teaspoons minced fresh chives	8 ounces crème fraîche, whipped
½ teaspoon salt	1½ teaspoons minced fresh chives
	Grated zest of 1 Meyer lemon
	4 ounces white sturgeon caviar

FOR THE CRÊPES

1. Mix the milk, eggs, and butter together. Sift in the flour and whisk thoroughly. Add the chives and salt.

2. Heat a nonstick 6-inch sauté pan over medium-high heat. Pour in enough batter to coat the bottom and cook until set, about one minute. Flip the crêpe, and cook the other side for 4 to 5 seconds. Be sure not to brown the crêpe. Repeat, stacking the crêpes on top of one another. The crêpes can be made ahead of time and refrigerated or frozen.

FOR THE SYRUP

Combine the water, sugar, and lemon juice in a saucepan and reduce to a thin syrup over medium heat. Remove from the heat and let cool to room temperature. The syrup will thicken as it cools.

TO SERVE

Place a small spoonful of whipped crème fraîche on each crêpe and sprinkle with some of the chives. Roll into a small package, and sprinkle with the zest. Serve topped with a small amount of the lemon syrup and a quenelle of the caviar.

CHARLIE TROTTER
RED SNAPPER CARPACCIO WITH BLOOD ORANGE JUICE, EXTRA-VIRGIN OLIVE OIL, AND LEMON THYME

The long-tailed red snapper is fabulous when consumed raw, but of course that means it has to be exceedingly fresh. Simply sliced, marinated in olive oil, drizzled with a little citrus juice, and perhaps strewn with some fresh lemon thyme leaves . . . it's hard to beat a preparation like this for simplicity and elegance. The fish literally melts in your mouth, with the olive oil providing an almost decadent richness. This is the perfect way to start a light warm-weather meal.

SERVES 4

VINAIGRETTE

3 tablespoons extra-virgin olive oil

¼ cup freshly squeezed blood orange juice

½ cup blood orange, cut into segments

12 thin slices skinless red snapper, each 4 x 2 inches (about 1 small fish)

Fleur de sel or sea salt

Grains of paradise in a peppermill

5 tablespoons extra-virgin olive oil

½ cup shaved fennel bulb

¼ cup freshly squeezed blood orange juice

Fennel pollen

1 teaspoon fresh lemon thyme leaves

FOR THE VINAIGRETTE

Combine the oil and the juice in a small bowl. Add the orange segments and let marinate for 15 minutes.

FOR THE SALAD

1. Season the snapper with salt and grains of paradise to taste, and rub with 3 tablespoons of the oil.

2. Season the shaved fennel with the juice, the remaining 2 tablespoons oil, and a pinch of salt.

3. Create a small mound of the shaved fennel in the center of each of 4 serving plates. Layer 3 slices of the snapper over the fennel salad. Place a few of the marinated orange segments around the snapper, and dress with about 2 tablespoons of the blood orange vinaigrette. Sprinkle fennel pollen on and around the snapper. Add a few grinds of grains of paradise and the lemon thyme leaves, and serve.

MARK MILITELLO
SALAD OF ROASTED BEETS, ASPARAGUS, AND QUAIL'S EGGS

The beauty of this dish is that it's colorful and earthy at the same time. Paradise Farms (near Homestead, Florida) supplies us with organic beets—all young and many of them heirloom—but if you don't have access to farm-fresh beets just use conventional beets and cut them into a ½-inch dice after cooking and cooling. We love delicate quail eggs, and sometimes you can find them at grocery or specialty stores. If you do, just cut them in half. If not, use hard-boiled hens' eggs: separate the yolks from the whites and grate them separately on a box grater until they look like small crumbles; then just sprinkle them on the salad.

SERVES 4

4 small to medium red or golden beets

Salt and freshly ground black pepper

1 tablespoon red wine vinegar

1 tablespoon extra-virgin olive oil

20 asparagus spears

4 quail's eggs

VINAIGRETTE

1 large shallot, cut into fine dice

2 tablespoons white wine vinegar

1 tablespoon freshly squeezed lemon juice

1 tablespoon freshly squeezed orange juice

Salt

¾ cup extra-virgin olive oil

1 tablespoon chopped fresh chervil

¼ teaspoon chopped lemon zest

¼ teaspoon chopped orange zest

4 handfuls frisée or mixed salad greens

1. Heat the oven to 400°F.

2. Wash and trim the beets. Put them in a baking dish, add a splash of water, and cover tightly. Roast the beets in the oven for about 45 minutes, or until they are cooked through and fork-tender. Allow the cooked beets to cool, uncovered.

3. Peel and cut the beets into wedges. Put them in a bowl and season generously with salt and pepper. Add the vinegar and oil, and toss gently. Set aside.

4. Bring a pot of salted water to a boil. Prepare an ice-water bath. Blanch the asparagus until crisp-tender; then transfer to the ice-water bath and leave until completely cooled. Place the asparagus on paper towels to dry, and set aside (reserve the ice-water bath).

5. Bring a small pot of water to a boil. Carefully lower the quail's eggs into the pot. Boil gently for 3 minutes. Transfer the eggs to the ice-water bath and let them cool completely. Peel and set aside.

FOR THE VINAIGRETTE

Put the shallot in a bowl and add the vinegar, the juices, and a pinch of salt. Let stand for 5 to 15 minutes. Then whisk in the oil, and stir in the chervil and zests. Taste for seasoning.

TO ASSEMBLE THE SALAD

Toss the frisée with a drizzle of the vinaigrette and arrange some on each of 4 salad plates. Next, create a bed with the asparagus; then add a few beet wedges. Top each salad with a quail egg that has been cut in half. (It should have a slightly undercooked center.) Drizzle all with another teaspoon of the vinaigrette.

GRILLED FOR ONE MINUTE
CHARLIE TROTTER

Q: What do you eat when no one is watching?

A: Chicago's famous Mr. Beef—although I would eat it while people were watching.

Q: What was your first food job and what did you learn?

A: I was a busboy at Ground Round when I was sixteen. I learned to be my own boss. That is, to have higher standards for myself than were even expected of me.

Q: Who is the one chef you would love to work with, alive or dead?

A: Chef Fernand Point of La Pyramide.

Q: What was the worst day so far in your career?

A: There are no bad days, because every day you learn something.

Q: What is your best advice to young chefs?

A: Read, read, read, and then read some more.

Q: What one character trait is most responsible for your success?

A: Sincerity of effort.

Q: Who or what was your earliest culinary inspiration?

A: Chef Louis Szathmary of The Bakery in Chicago.

Q: What's your favorite off-hours pastime?

A: Reading, reading, reading, and more reading.

> "AS AN EARLY FOODIE (BEFORE THE WORD WAS INVENTED), I AM AMAZED, AMUSED, AND EVEN TERRIFIED TO SEE THE FERVOR OF AMERICA'S OBSESSION WITH FOOD ACTED OUT EVERY YEAR ON THE BEACH AT THE SOUTH BEACH WINE & FOOD FESTIVAL. I LOVED BEING IN THE MIDDLE OF IT ALL."
>
> —GAEL GREENE, AUTHOR AND RESTAURANT CRITIC, INSATIABLECRITIC.COM

NOBU MATSUHISA AND THOMAS BUCKLEY
BLACK COD IN BUTTER LETTUCE WRAPS

I have so many happy memories from participating in the festival over the years! I couldn't be there in 2009, but Thomas Buckley, my executive chef from Nobu Miami Beach, was on hand, serving dishes from *Nobu Miami: The Party Cookbook*. This dish, one of our signatures, was a huge hit. In the restaurant we serve the black cod as an entrée, but for parties and special events we do this finger-food version, which is extremely popular. Even if I make 500 portions, it disappears faster than any other dish! The flavors are deep and intense, but the lettuce wrapping lends a light, fresh touch.

SERVES 10

1 to 2 fillets black cod, skin on (12 ounces total), cut into 10 squares

10 teaspoons Nobu-Style Saikyo Miso (recipe follows)

10 pieces Garlic Chips (recipe follows)

2 ounces frozen kataifi dough, deep-fried

10 leaves butter lettuce, washed and crisped in cold water

1 thumb-size knob fresh ginger, peeled and slivered

1. Sear the skin side of the cod squares under a salamander or broiler; turn over, spread with the Saikyo Miso, and sear until the color changes.

2. Break the Garlic Chips and kataifi dough into the lettuce leaves. Top with the cod and slivered ginger. Then wrap the lettuce around the filling.

NOBU-STYLE SAIKYO MISO

MAKES 3 CUPS

⅔ cup sake

⅔ cup mirin

1⅔ cups white miso

1⅛ cups sugar

1. In a medium saucepan, bring the sake and mirin to a boil over high heat to evaporate the alcohol.

2. Turn the heat to low and add the miso, mixing with a wooden spoon. When the miso has dissolved completely, turn the heat up to high and add the sugar, stirring constantly with the wooden spoon to prevent scorching. When the sugar has dissolved completely and the mixture becomes a smooth paste, remove from the heat and cool to room temperature.

GARLIC CHIPS

MAKES 1 CUP

3 cups canola oil

10 cloves garlic, thinly sliced on a mandoline

1 cup whole milk

1. Heat the oil to 300°F in a skillet.

2. Place the garlic and milk in a saucepan and bring to a boil (to remove any bitterness). After a few seconds, remove the garlic. Wash in cold water and pat dry.

3. Deep-fry the garlic slices in the oil over low heat. When they turn light golden, immediately transfer them to a paper-lined dish (they will continue to cook).

DANIEL BOULUD
MELON SALAD WITH LEMONGRASS SHRIMP

The simplicity of this dish, perfect for a summer lunch, is deceptive. There's a great contrast of sweetness and acidity from the melon and the limes, along with unexpected layers of flavor from the basil, cilantro, and lemongrass.

SERVES 4

1½ pounds large shrimp, peeled and deveined

6 tablespoons extra-virgin olive oil

2 teaspoons finely grated peeled ginger

2 teaspoons finely chopped lemongrass

Juice of 2 limes

Finely grated zest of 1 lime

⅛ teaspoon Tabasco sauce

Salt and freshly ground white pepper

1 ripe honeydew melon

1 ripe small, round red watermelon

1 tablespoon finely chopped fresh purple basil, plus additional small leaves

1 tablespoon finely chopped fresh cilantro, plus additional small leaves

1. In a medium saucepan of boiling salted water, cook the shrimp for 3 to 5 minutes. Drain. When cool enough to handle, slice in half lengthwise.

2. In a small bowl, whisk together the oil, ginger, lemongrass, lime juice, zest, and Tabasco. Season the dressing to taste with salt and pepper. Set aside.

3. Cut the honeydew and watermelon in half, cut away the rind, and remove the seeds. Cut the melons into ⅛-inch-thick slices. Remove the watermelon seeds (it's okay if the slices don't stay intact). Using a cake ring or a glass that is slightly smaller than the mouth of a 12- to 16-ounce martini glass or Champagne coupe, cut out 16 slices from the watermelon and 16 slices from the honeydew. Save the nicest 4 watermelon slices for the top.

4. Set out four martini glasses or Champagne coupes. In each glass, layer 2 slices of watermelon and honeydew, lightly sprinkling each melon layer with some dressing, basil, cilantro, and salt and pepper to taste. (You may need to trim the melon slices so they fit neatly into the glasses, which should be half full at this point.) Divide the shrimp among the glasses, arranging them in concentric circles. Season the shrimp with some dressing, basil, cilantro, salt, and pepper. Layer the glasses with honeydew, then the watermelon, seasoning each layer as before. Top each salad with a reserved watermelon slice, and sprinkle lightly with dressing, basil, cilantro, salt, and pepper. Garnish each salad with a basil leaf and a cilantro leaf. Refrigerate for at least 1 hour before serving (the melon and shrimp taste best when well chilled).

TOM COLICCHIO
CARAMELIZED TOMATO TARTS

Here's a twist on the classic apple tarte Tatin, using roasted tomatoes in place of apples. Use greenmarket or farm-stand tomatoes if possible; either way, you'll find that roasting intensifies the flavor. The onion confit can last for weeks in the fridge, so make use of the extra. Adding sherry vinegar to the caramelized sugar cuts down the sweetness of the caramel. I love this tart on its own or as a garnish for roasted lamb.

SERVES 4

4 tablespoons sugar

1 tablespoon water

¼ teaspoon sherry vinegar

4 roasted garlic cloves (recipe follows)

12 Niçoise olives, pitted

4 roasted tomato halves (recipe follows)

Kosher salt and freshly ground black pepper

1 to 1½ cups Onion Confit (recipe follows)

8 ounces frozen puff pastry, defrosted

1. Heat the oven to 425°F.

2. In a small saucepan, combine the sugar with the water, and heat over medium heat, swirling the pan until the sugar has completely dissolved. Then let the mixture boil, swirling occasionally, until the resulting caramel is nut-brown. Remove the saucepan from the heat. Add the vinegar to the caramel, swirling the pan until thoroughly combined.

3. Pour the caramel into four 4-ounce ramekins. Allow the caramel to cool for 1 minute or so. Then place 1 garlic clove, 3 olives, and a tomato half into each of 4 ramekins. Add salt and pepper to taste, and top with the onion confit.

4. Cut the pastry into rounds that are slightly larger than the opening of the ramekins (these will become the tart crusts). Place the pastry rounds over the onion confit. Then transfer the ramekins to a baking sheet and bake until the pastry is puffed and golden, about 20 minutes. Allow the tarts to cool for 1 to 2 minutes, then carefully turn them out onto plates. Serve warm or at room temperature.

recipe continues

ONION CONFIT

MAKES ABOUT 3 CUPS

2 tablespoons extra-virgin olive oil

6 onions, thinly sliced (about 12 cups)

Kosher salt and freshly ground black pepper

1 cup chicken stock

2 tablespoons white wine vinegar

2 tablespoons fresh thyme leaves

4 anchovy fillets, chopped (optional)

1. In a large deep skillet set over medium heat, heat the oil until it slides easily across the pan. Add the onions, and season with salt and pepper. Reduce the heat to medium-low and cook, stirring occasionally, for about 30 minutes, or until the onions are very soft but not brown.

2. Add the stock and vinegar and simmer, continuing to stir occasionally, until the pan is dry and the onions are golden, about 30 minutes more.

3. Add the thyme leaves and anchovies, if using, and mix well. Serve warm or at room temperature. The confit should be refrigerated and will last at least a week.

FERRAN ADRIÀ
CARROT AIR WITH BITTER COCONUT MILK

I created carrot air in 2003, as a tapas-appetizer to be served at cool room temperature. That was the year I was heavily inspired by nature and the essential elements of our planet, including earth, air, sea, and snow. . . and that was the year that "airs" were born. As bitter almonds are not readily available in the U.S., you can use regular almonds instead. The coconut powder should be easy to find, but you could substitute unsweetened coconut milk, found at Asian specialty stores, for the bitter coconut milk. To serve, use six small crystal bowls or glasses.

SERVES 6

10 large carrots (about 7 ounces each), trimmed

2½ ounces coconut powder (found in Asian markets)

4 ounces water

¾ ounce bitter almonds

Madras curry powder

1. Using a juicer, liquefy the carrots; refrigerate until ready to use.

2. In a bowl, mix the coconut powder with the water to obtain a homogenous coconut milk. Rough-chop the almonds and then use an immersion blender to blend the almonds and milk. Let the milk and almonds infuse for 20 minutes, and then strain the milk through a Superbag strainer into a container. Keep the bitter coconut milk in the refrigerator.

3. To make the carrot air, put the carrot juice in a deep rectangular dish (to allow more surface area for frothing), and froth with a hand or immersion blender by touching just the surface.

4. Place 1 tablespoon of the bitter coconut milk in each bowl or glass. On top of the milk, sprinkle some curry powder. With a big spoon, collect the top of the carrot air and place on top to reach 1½ inches over the rim.

GEORGE DURAN
GRANNY SMITH GUACAMOLE kid friendly

I could eat guac all day. But aren't you tired of the same old mushy versions? Whip up this crunchier alternative and watch how your friends and family light up when they bite into the juicy tart pieces of Granny Smith apple. They'll never guess what genius move you made to turn this classic favorite into a surprising treat.

SERVES 8 TO 10

3 ripe avocados, halved and pitted

½ cup finely chopped Vidalia onion

½ cup snipped fresh cilantro

Juice of 1 lime

Tabasco sauce

1 Granny Smith apple, peeled, cored, and finely chopped

Kosher salt or table salt

Assorted dippers (such as baked fruit crisps, apple chips, and/or tortilla chips)

1. Scoop the avocado flesh into a bowl and add the onion, cilantro, juice, and Tabasco to taste. Mash with a fork until the desired consistency is reached. Then fold in the apple and season with salt.

2. Serve with dippers of choice on the side.

"BEING HONORED AT SOUTH BEACH WAS ONE OF THE MOST EMOTIONAL MOMENTS I'VE EVER EXPERIENCED. THESE WERE MAGICAL DAYS FOR ME AND MY WIFE."

—FERRAN ADRIÀ

ALICE WATERS
GRAPEFRUIT AND AVOCADO SALAD

I like to serve this refreshing salad in the late winter and early spring, when citrus is at its best and avocados are perfectly ripe. You can serve it as a first course or to revive the palate between the main course and dessert.

SERVES 4

2 medium ruby grapefruit

1 teaspoon white wine vinegar

Salt and freshly ground black pepper

2 tablespoons extra-virgin olive oil

2 medium Hass avocados, cut in half and pits removed

Fresh chervil

1. With a sharp knife, peel the grapefruit down to the flesh, removing all the rind and pith. Cut the sections free, slicing carefully along the partitioning membranes, and set them aside. Squeeze the juice from the membranes. Measure 2 tablespoons of the juice into a small bowl.

2. Stir the vinegar into the juice, and season with salt and pepper. Whisk in the oil. Taste, and adjust the acid and salt.

3. Peel the avocado halves and cut them into ¼-inch slices. Sprinkle lightly with salt. Arrange the grapefruit sections and avocado slices alternately on a plate, and spoon the vinaigrette over. Garnish with chervil, and serve.

"MY FAVORITE FESTIVAL MEMORY IS WHEN ALICE WATERS PRESENTED JAMIE OLIVER WITH OUR LIFETIME ACHIEVEMENT AWARD IN 2008. ALICE TOOK THE STAGE TO SAY A FEW VERY MOVING WORDS ABOUT JAMIE'S WORK. THEN JAMIE, BEAMING FROM HEAD TO TOE, BOUNDED UP TO ACCEPT THE AWARD AND GAVE ALICE A HUGE HUG. IT WAS AN ELECTRIC MOMENT, AND YOU REALLY COULD FEEL THE LOVE THAT THESE TWO HAVE FOR FOOD AND FOR HUMANITY."

—JAIE LAPLANTE, ASSOCIATE DIRECTOR, SBWFF

MICHELLE BERNSTEIN
SMOKED HAM AND CHEESE *CROQUETAS*

I love tapas and how they encourage sharing and socializing. I demoed these at SoBe and serve them in my restaurants as well. They're my best seller—people go crazy! They're not like the typical *croquetas* you find on 8th Street in Miami; they're lush, cheesy, and studded with smoky ham. Serve a bunch of them on crumpled-up parchment paper with dishes of fig or strawberry marmalade. And whatever you do, don't give your guests forks—they should eat with their fingers! These go beautifully with sangria (red or white), Albariño, or beer. Enjoy!

SERVES 4 TO 6

4 tablespoons olive oil, plus more for frying

1 cup minced yellow onion

1 cup plus 4 tablespoons all-purpose flour

1 cup milk

4 ounces Gorgonzola dolce or any creamy blue cheese

6 ounces *jamón serrano* or smoked ham, sliced paper-thin, julienned, and cut into ¼-inch pieces

Salt and freshly ground black pepper

1 large egg, beaten

2 cups dry bread crumbs (Japanese panko if available)

Fig or orange marmalade

1. Heat the 4 tablespoons oil in a saucepan set over medium heat. Add the onions and cook, stirring, until soft and transparent, about 5 minutes.

2. Stir in the 4 tablespoons flour and cook for about 1 minute; then whisk in the milk. Cook, stirring constantly, until thick.

3. Stir in the cheese until it has completely melted. Stir in the *jamón* and season with salt and pepper. Spread the mixture onto a baking sheet. Refrigerate until it sets, about 30 minutes.

4. Place the remaining 1 cup flour in a dish, the beaten egg in another dish, and the bread crumbs in another dish. Form the chilled batter into little 2-inch-long cylinders. Dip each *croqueta* first in the flour, then in the egg, and finally in the bread crumbs, making sure every area is covered with crumbs, using your hands to crust the *croquetas* well. Chill in the refrigerator for 1 hour. (The breaded *croquetas* can be frozen in an airtight bag for up to 1 month. Do not defrost before frying.)

5. Pour oil into a large, deep, heavy-bottomed frying pan to a depth of 3 inches. Heat the oil to 350°F. Fry 4 to 5 *croquetas* at a time until golden. Using a slotted spoon, carefully transfer them to paper towels to drain. Serve immediately, with fig or orange marmalade for dipping.

"LEE AND HIS TEAM ARE WHAT I CALL FAMILY. THEY ARE THE MOST DELICIOUS, BEAUTIFUL, PATIENT PEOPLE IN THE WORLD. WE AS CHEFS WAIT UNTIL THE LAST MINUTE FOR EVERYTHING. WE'RE NEEDY PEOPLE AND UNPREDICTABLE. BUT THEY NEVER EVER LOSE THEIR PATIENCE OR THEIR TEMPER WITH US. THEY SHOULD ALL GET A MEDAL!"

—MICHELLE BERNSTEIN

GORDON MAYBURY
BAKED KATAIFI-WRAPPED GOAT CHEESE

This was one of the hors d'oeuvres at the Tribute Dinner honoring Emeril Lagasse at the Loews Miami Beach in 2009. We chose this as a vegetarian option, but it's really the perfect canapé: it's crunchy and bite-size, and the warm, tangy, salty goat cheese simply explodes in your mouth. And it goes so well with Champagne!

MAKES 35

1 pound goat cheese

1 cup mixture of finely diced carrot, celery, and onion

1 package frozen kataifi dough, defrosted

Unsalted butter, melted

1. Heat the oven to 425°F.

2. In a bowl, mix the cheese and vegetables together. Set aside.

3. Pull off a piece of kataifi, and spread it out to measure 1 x 4 inches. Brush it with melted butter. Roll some of the cheese mixture into a 1 x ½-inch cylinder, and wrap it up in the dough. Repeat with the remaining filling and kataifi.

4. Bake on a baking sheet for about 15 minutes, or until golden brown. Remove from the oven and serve warm.

ANITA LO
CHILLED CRAB AND CORN CHAWAN MUSHI

This is my Japanese take on classic American summertime flavors, served at SoBe in 2007. Most of these Asian products can be found at Whole Foods, in specialty stores, or online. If you have trouble finding fresh shiso, substitute a generous pinch of finely chopped fresh tarragon or mint leaves.

SERVES 4

CHAWAN MUSHI

1 cup dashi

1 large egg, beaten

1 tablespoon soy sauce

1½ tablespoons mirin

Salt and freshly ground black pepper

CORN SALAD

⅓ cup corn kernels, blanched

2 shiso leaves, cut into small squares

1 tablespoon vegetable, canola, or soy oil

Salt and freshly ground black pepper

CRAB SALAD

6 ounces jumbo lump crabmeat

Freshly squeezed lemon juice, to taste

Pinch of grated lemon zest

Salt and freshly ground black pepper

1 tablespoon julienned scallion greens

FOR THE CHAWAN MUSHI

Mix the dashi and egg together. Add the soy sauce and mirin, and season with salt and pepper. Divide among 4 ramekins, cover with plastic wrap, and steam in a water bath for about 18 minutes, or until set. Remove, and refrigerate for 2 to 3 minutes.

FOR THE CORN SALAD

Mix the corn, shiso, and oil together. Season with salt and pepper. Spoon the salad over the chilled chawan mushi.

FOR THE CRAB SALAD

Mix the crabmeat, lemon juice, and zest together, and season with salt and pepper. Taste, and adjust the seasonings.

TO SERVE

Top the corn salad with the crab. Garnish with a few scallions, and serve chilled.

ALLEN SUSSER
WILD FLORIDA SHRIMP MOJITO

This is my personal twist on the classic mojito, made with good rum, lime, and mint. I use locally caught wild Florida shrimp, but feel free to use any fresh shrimp, then splash it with the mojito fixings. It's like a tropical vacation on a plate—colorful, sultry, and delicious. In fact, a chilled Cuban mojito is a perfect match. This dish was a huge hit at the festival in 2004; we ran through 1,500 portions in less than two hours!

SERVES 4

4 teaspoons olive oil

16 jumbo Florida shrimp, peeled and deveined

1 teaspoon minced garlic

¼ teaspoon ground cumin

1½ teaspoons kosher salt

1 teaspoon freshly ground black pepper

3 tablespoons dark rum

2 tablespoons freshly squeezed lime juice

1 tablespoon chopped fresh mint

½ cup chopped fresh cilantro, plus sprigs for garnish

¼ cup minced red onion

1 cup diced avocado

1 large orange, peeled and segmented

1 tablespoon minced jalapeño

1. In a large sauté pan, warm the oil. Add the shrimp, and stir in the garlic and cumin. Season with 1 teaspoon salt and ½ teaspoon pepper. Cook over high heat for 1 minute, then reduce the heat and turn the shrimp. Carefully add the rum and then the lime juice. Continue to cook the shrimp until they are rosy pink. Toss the shrimp with the mint and 2 tablespoons of the cilantro, and set aside.

2. In a small stainless-steel bowl, combine the onion, remaining 6 tablespoons cilantro, avocado, orange segments, and jalapeño, and season with the remaining salt and pepper. Toss lightly.

3. Spoon the salsa into the center of each plate. Arrange the shrimp around the salsa. Drizzle with mojito sauce (the pan juices) and garnish with cilantro sprigs.

"THE BEAUTY OF THE FESTIVAL IS SEEING SO MANY OF MY CHEF FRIENDS AND MEETING SOME OF THE NEWEST TALENT ALL AT THE SAME TIME."

—ALLEN SUSSER

MARC EHRLER
CHILLED SCALLOP AND LYCHEE MARTINI

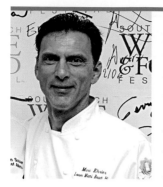

In 2005, Emeril and I hosted a winemaker dinner and served it beneath the stars. Fabulous! This was the most popular starter. With its tropical influences, it really reflects the Floribbean-Latino heritage of Miami, as well as the diversity of our ingredients. (Local farmers hand-selected the lychees for me, to be sure they were just perfect!) If you can't wait a week for your vanilla oil, simply warm the oil with the vanilla in it and let it rest for two hours before using.

MAKES 10

6 ounces dry-pack scallops, cut into small dice

4 ounces lychee, cut into small dice

1 teaspoon chopped fresh chives

1 teaspoon chopped fresh cilantro

¼ teaspoon chopped shallot

1 large egg yolk

2 tablespoons Dijon mustard

½ cup plus 2 tablespoons Vanilla Oil (recipe follows)

¼ teaspoon sherry vinegar

Salt and freshly ground black pepper

1. In a bowl, combine the scallops, lychee, chives, cilantro, and shallot.

2. In a separate bowl, combine the egg yolk and mustard. Slowly drizzle in the vanilla oil, whisking constantly until it reaches a light mayonnaise consistency. Add the vinegar.

3. Mix the mayonnaise and the seafood combination together until well coated. Season with salt and pepper. Serve ice-cold in mini martini glasses.

VANILLA OIL

Split some vanilla beans in half and scoop out the seeds (reserve the seeds for another use). Place the beans in a dry container, cover with canola oil, and let infuse, tightly covered, for 1 week.

ERIC RIPERT
THINLY SLICED HAMACHI MARINATED PERUVIAN-STYLE WITH COCONUT FLAKES

Hamachi has a buttery, melting texture, and its rich density is highlighted by the silkiness of the coconut milk. This ceviche is rich in spice, and the acidity brings a freshness to the hamachi. If hamachi isn't available, use a similarly dense fish such as mahimahi or striped bass.

SERVES 4

8 ounces hamachi

¼ cup unsweetened coconut milk

6 tablespoons freshly squeezed lime juice

4 tablespoons extra-virgin olive oil

1 teaspoon hot sauce

2 tablespoons julienned red onion

1 tablespoon brunoise tomato (¼-inch dice of peeled, seeded tomato)

1 teaspoon minced jalapeño

2 tablespoons julienned fresh cilantro

2 teaspoons julienned fresh mint

2 teaspoons julienned fresh basil

Fine sea salt and freshly ground white pepper

½ cup unsweetened coconut flakes, toasted

12 micro cilantro sprouts

Piment d'Espelette

1. Slice the hamachi as thin as possible, and reserve the slices in the refrigerator.

2. Prepare the marinade by combining the coconut milk, lime juice, oil, hot sauce, onion, tomato, jalapeño, cilantro, mint, and basil in a bowl.

3. When ready to serve, season the fish with salt and pepper. Add the fish to the marinade. Mix well and marinate for 2 minutes.

4. Divide the ceviche among 4 small bowls. Spoon 1 tablespoon marinade over each portion. Garnish the top of each ceviche with 3 micro cilantro sprouts, a sprinkling of coconut flakes, and some Piment d'Espelette. Serve immediately.

> **"THE FESTIVAL SEEMS TO BE AN ACCUMULATION OF MINI MIRACLES—BUT ITS SUCCESS IS DUE TO THE INCREDIBLE ORGANIZATION BEHIND THE SCENES: SO MUCH DISCIPLINE, PASSION, TALENT, AND LEADERSHIP."**

—ERIC RIPERT

CHAPTER 3
BARBECUE

The year was 2002, the first year of the fest, and I wanted to do a beach barbecue. And I got it into my head that Champagne would be just the thing to go with it. So off I went to see my friends at Moët & Chandon, to ask them to be the event sponsor.

Their response was anything but bubbly.

They were like, "Ah, we don't know if this is something we want to do." But I told them, "I think this is *exactly* what you want to do: to send the message that Champagne isn't just for anniversaries and Valentine's Day."

Little by little, they came around, offering to donate both Champagne and money—and the BubbleQ was born.

That first year Steven Raichlen—a cookbook author and true barbecue maniac—hosted the event, gathered all the chefs, and did the hors d'oeuvres poolside at the Delano Hotel before we moved out onto the beach. We had no fancy tent—just lots of tables, five chefs at grill stations, and a huge bonfire under the stars.

"We feasted on the smokiest brisket from Oklahoma," Steven remembers, "the most crackling-crisp hog from West Virginia, and whole salmons roasted around bonfires the way the Pacific Northwest Indians have done it for thousands of years."

I recall the image of that salmon being cooked around that fire as just magical, and our guests felt the same way.

The BubbleQ immediately became our signature event. Each year, all 2,000

THE PERFECT STORM

REMEMBER THE BOOK AND THE MOVIE *THE PERFECT STORM,* NAMED FOR THAT RARE COMBINATION OF CIRCUMSTANCES THAT CREATES THE MOTHER OF ALL STORMS, A DELUGE OF EPIC PROPORTIONS? AT SOBE WE HAD OUR OWN VERSION IN 2006. OUR IMMENSELY CAPABLE (AND FUNNY) SOBE MANAGING DIRECTOR, DEVIN PADGETT, WAS AT THE BUBBLEQ WHEN IT HIT, AND HERE'S HOW HE REMEMBERS IT.

"Okay, so we check the weather and we hear it's going to be *partly cloudy.* And there we are, two thousand or so people all dressed up on the beach eating ribs when this quasi hurricane . . . this microburst . . . this God shot . . . hits. One minute we're merrily *whatever* and the next it's a Stephen King movie. In two seconds . . . nightmare! Bang! I catch two Champagne flutes flying through the air. Beautiful people are running screaming from the beach wearing one high heel . . . people are laying on the ground, auction items are getting trashed, there's chaos, commotion. For a few minutes there, it was the end of the world! In fact, I heard the Doors in my head singing 'This is the Ennnnnnd.' I'm laughing now but it was scary . . . all these fancy hairdos whipping around and barbecue sandwiches flying. We had these transgendered showgirls dancing onstage, and in two seconds they were a complete mess, like wet dogs. They were like *Where are we?* There were light towers falling and embers flying around in tents. You couldn't have scripted it any better. My most-lasting image of that evening will be flying down the beach in my Bobcat, as fast as I could, getting lashed with rain from all sides, with Dean and Lynae Fearing laughing psychotically beside me like it was the best joyride in the world.

"When I first started at SoBe in 2003, I kept asking, 'What's your rain contingency?' And the answer was always 'Oh Devin, this is South Florida! It *never* rains in South Florida in February!' Well it turns out it does, which is why the BubbleQ and the Burger Bash are now held in a 100- by 300-foot tent. The End."

BubbleQ tickets sell out in a flash and then immediately start popping up on eBay and Craigslist. As the event gets closer, people routinely offer us two and three times face value, hoping to score a ticket.

Each year we select one big name to "host" BubbleQ. That chef, in turn, names other chefs he or she would like us to invite to cook. After a bit of back-and-forth, twenty to twenty-five chefs are selected. And I'm proud to say by now we've hosted most of the finest pit masters in the country.

But any new endeavor has its learning curve—and the BubbleQ's was *huge.* "Did we make grand mistakes along the way? Absolutely!" says Kelly Murphy, one of our two BubbleQ event managers.

My colleague at Southern Wine & Spirits, Brett Dunne, remembers that first year with a laugh: "We thought we had all our bases covered," he says. "We had buckets and ice and glasses and signage. We had two-hundred-plus cases of Champagne. What nobody anticipated was how we were going to wheel hand trucks piled with heavy cases of Champagne across the sand. But we made a human chain and got them where they needed to go."

Then there was the year we had these big inflatable bars, which were very cool-looking and surprisingly sturdy, as long as no one tripped on a power cord. Of course the bar top was completely covered with Champagne glasses and ice buckets when it happened. Yep—the whole thing went down like a huge deflating AeroBed.

And who could forget that fifty-two-foot NBC *Today* show production trailer, filled with 50,000 pounds of equipment, wheels spinning for what seemed like an eternity, stuck in the soft sand?

One year, forty-five minutes before the

BubbleQ started, 200 pounds of marinated, seasoned Kobe beef cheeks tumbled into the sand. "They were completely *breaded* in sand," remembers Elaina Moran, another SoBe event manager. "So the manager of the Forge ran back to his restaurant and got short ribs and saved the day. Of course, the food was great."

Thinking back on ten years of 'cue, so many powerful images come to mind!

I loved how Myron Mixon of Jack's Old South schlepped those two 245-pound butchered hogs down with him from Unadilla, Georgia, then stayed up all night

THE BEST WINES FOR BARBECUE

WHEN IT COMES TO PAIRING WINE WITH BARBECUE, THE POSSIBILITIES ARE AS LIMITLESS AS THE MEATS, SEAFOODS, AND VEGGIES YOU CAN SIZZLE, SMOKE, AND SAUCE UP. TO MAKE A REALLY SMOKIN' MATCH, ANDREA ROBINSON, MASTER SOMMELIER AND AUTHOR OF *GREAT WINE MADE SIMPLE,* SUGGESTS KEEPING THESE GUIDELINES IN MIND.

IF THERE'S BODY: If your core ingredient is light-bodied—say, oysters or corn on the cob—go with a lighter-bodied white wine or a light red such as Pinot Noir or Beaujolais. If the main ingredient has more body—like brisket or ribeye—a heavier red will best stand up to the heft of the meat. Look for California Cabs, Washington Merlots and Syrahs, Argentinian Malbecs, Spanish Rioja gran reserva, and Piedmont or Tuscan reds from Italy.

IF THERE'S SWEETNESS, such as a sugary sauce: Choose carefully because sweetness in the dish can make a dry wine taste out of balance and sour. The whites that work are those with a hint of sweetness, such as white Zinfandel, Riesling Spätlese, French Alsace Pinot Gris, demi-sec sparkling wine and Champagne (yep!), and Torrontes from Argentina. For reds, go with super-ripe styles whose succulent dark fruit is a great foil for a sweet sauce: California Zinfandel and Syrah, or Aussie Shiraz and Grenache are delicious choices.

IF THERE'S TANGINESS, such as a vinegary sauce: Go with wines that have plenty of their own lively, tangy acidity. The dueling acids in the sauce and the wine will actually tone each other down, letting the wine's fruit and the dish's flavors emerge. For starters, why not host your own BubbleQ and pour brut or rosé sparkling wine or Champagne? Other really good white and rosé choices include New Zealand Sauvignon Blanc, Italian Pinot Grigio, French Sancerre, Spanish Albariño, Spanish Rioja rosé, or French Provençal rosé. For reds, Italian Chianti and Barbera and Oregon Pinot Noir are great choices.

IF THERE'S SPICY HEAT AND A LITTLE TINGLE ON THE TONGUE: No problem! A touch of sweetness will tame it. Look for any of the selections mentioned above in the section "If there's sweetness," keeping in mind that the chill of the whites and blush wines will offer a little extra relief. You can also try a chillable red such as Beaujolais Nouveau or Spanish Rioja crianza. And maybe the best bet of all? Italian Moscato d'Asti—it's served cool and is slightly sweet, bubbly, and low in alcohol.

on the beach tending his massive smoker with a mountain of hickory and peach wood. Twenty-seven hours of cooking time!

I loved the year when we served Champagne in the mini individual bottles and everyone sipped with straws.

And then of course there was the year that Willie Nelson performed. BubbleQ tickets had already sold out by the time we confirmed his band—but when we got the chance to get Willie, how could we resist?

And who among us will *ever* forget the deluge of 2006? It was the worst storm I remember in thirty years in Miami. The rain came down in huge sloppy sheets and 2,000 guests ran for cover or crammed themselves into our tiny chef-station tents. Restaurateur Drew Nieporent remembers huddling there, elbow to elbow, Champagne bottles being passed back and forth, and looking down to see water under his feet. "I've never ever seen rain pooling on sand before or since," he says.

When the first hungry guests surge into the massive BubbleQ tent on the Friday night of festival weekend, they see twenty-plus well-known smiling chefs in pristine chef coats flanked by eager student helpers . . . and a phalanx of handsome bartenders lining up a battalion of Champagne flutes. They smell delectable barbecue sizzling, the aromas of wood smoke, charcoal, live flame, and juicy meat. They hear music, laughter, and maybe even the ocean.

But little do they know how much work is involved in making our dreamy beach barbecue a reality. Much of the heavy lifting, food-wise, is done by the hospitality students at Florida International University (FIU). And leading the student brigade are two of the most dedicated and passionate people I know: Michael Moran and Kelly

Murphy. Michael runs the back of the house and Kelly runs the front. Or as Kelly puts it: "Mike is the culinary manager and I'm the event manager and together we're the bomb."

I couldn't have said it better.

All BubbleQ food is prepped at the Miami Beach Convention Center, with its 200,000-square-foot kitchen—the largest in the city. It's actually three separate kitchens, and the chefs use golf carts and bikes to move between them.

For three solid days in the lead-up to Friday night, 175 FIU students work there around the clock, readying 22,500 portions of food. In terms of raw ingredients, that means 1.5 tons of beef and pork, 1 ton of seafood, 2 tons of produce, and more.

By the time each celebrity chef shows up in Miami, his assigned team of six student helpers know his dish down to the smallest detail, and the bulk of his prep has been done (if requested). "I'm just amazed by the festival staff and the students," says chef Dean Fearing, veteran of many BubbleQs. "Everyone goes above and beyond to see that we have everything we need. Mike Moran rocks!"

"One year at the BubbleQ," chef Paul Bartolotta remembers, "I was knee-deep in sand with an army of volunteers, thinking, "Why are they all so excited about helping me cut hundreds of pounds of langoustines?" The students' enthusiasm totally enriched the experience for me."

BubbleQ guests will consume 4,000 bottles of Champagne during the three-hour party. And it's not just any Champagne, mind you, but none other than Perrier-Jouët, which replaced Moët & Chandon as event sponsor in 2009.

So let's get on with it! Here are some irresistible barbecue dishes from a few of our favorite BubbleQ chefs.

JON ASHTON
MISO-GLAZED SEA BASS WITH SOY REDUCTION AND PICKLED CUCUMBER SALAD

People usually think of meats when barbecuing, but for the BubbleQ I decided to go with sea bass instead. Its firm yet moist white flesh holds up well on the grill, and it has a delicate yet flavorful taste. I kept it simple and fun, using miso as a glaze for sweetness. Normally I like to serve it on steamed jasmine rice with Asian stir-fried vegetables. At the BubbleQ, however, I chose pickled cucumber salad, adding a refreshing component to counter SoBe's sizzling weather.

SERVES 6

⅓ cup sake

⅓ cup mirin

⅓ cup light yellow miso paste

2½ tablespoons (packed) dark brown sugar

2 tablespoons soy sauce

6 6-ounce sea bass fillets, each thinly sliced into 3 2-ounce slices

Soy Reduction (recipe follows)

Pickled Cucumber Salad (recipe follows)

1. In a shallow glass baking dish, combine the sake, mirin, miso, sugar, and soy sauce. Add the fish and turn to coat. Cover and refrigerate for at least 48 hours.

2. Heat a grill or a frying pan to medium-high.

3. Remove the fish from the marinade. Grill for about 6 minutes, 3 minutes per side, until just opaque in the center.

4. Place the sea bass on serving plates, drizzle with Soy Reduction, and serve with Pickled Cucumber Salad.

SOY REDUCTION

1 pound dark brown sugar

1 cup soy sauce

¼ cup chicken stock

2 cloves garlic, cut in half

2 whole star anise

1 cinnamon stick (about 3 inches long)

1. In a saucepan, bring the sugar, soy sauce, stock, garlic, star anise, and cinnamon to a boil. Simmer until the mixture coats the back of a spoon.

2. Strain; discard the spices. Set aside.

PICKLED CUCUMBER SALAD

2 cups thinly sliced Japanese cucumbers

1 teaspoon salt

¼ cup rice vinegar

1 tablespoon soy sauce

1 tablespoon sugar

1 teaspoon Asian sesame oil

1. In a large bowl, combine the cucumbers and salt, and mix well. Add the vinegar, soy sauce, sugar, and sesame oil, and mix well. Let marinate for 20 minutes before serving.

2. Adjust the seasonings before serving.

"BARBECUE IN AMERICA HAS A BEAUTIFUL WAY OF BRINGING EVERYONE INTO THE BACK GARDEN. I LOVE IT, ABSOLUTELY LOVE IT. THERE'S NOTHING BETTER THAN EVERYONE STANDING AROUND THE GRILL . . . THE ANTICIPATION, THE CRISPY AND CRUNCHY, THE SMOKE AND THE SMELL. BACK HOME IN ENGLAND, WE CAN'T BARBECUE BECAUSE SUMMER VISITS FOR ONLY ONE DAY EACH YEAR. LAST YEAR IN LIVERPOOL, FOR EXAMPLE, SUMMER CAME ON A WEDNESDAY. NO WONDER WHY I LOVE IT HERE, AND WHY I LOVE THE BUBBLEQ!"

—JON ASHTON

EMERIL LAGASSE
SAMBAL SHRIMP

Inspired by Thai flavors, this is a quick, spicy grilled dish that is sure to please a crowd. The mint and cilantro add a cooling element to the heat and spice of the shrimp. Pair it with an ice-cold beer and you'll be in the zone!

SERVES 6 TO 8

2 cups sambal oelek (Indonesian-style chile sauce)

½ cup sugar

½ cup freshly squeezed lime juice

½ cup olive oil

¼ cup minced garlic

¼ cup minced peeled fresh ginger

¼ cup mirin

2 tablespoons fish sauce

2 tablespoons dark sesame oil

3 pounds U-10 head-on shrimp, peeled and deveined, head and tail segments left intact

2 tablespoons roughly chopped fresh cilantro

2 tablespoons roughly chopped fresh mint

1. In a medium bowl, combine the sambal, sugar, lime juice, olive oil, garlic, ginger, mirin, fish sauce, and sesame oil, and whisk well. Let stand at room temperature for at least 1 hour and up to 4 hours.

2. Place the shrimp and all but ½ cup of the marinade in a 1-gallon resealable plastic food storage bag. Reserve the remaining marinade. Let the shrimp marinate for 1 hour.

3. Heat a grill to medium-high.

4. Remove the shrimp from the marinade. Place the shrimp on the grill and cook until they are just cooked through, 2 to 2½ minutes per side.

5. Place the shrimp in a large bowl and add the reserved ½ cup marinade along with the cilantro and mint. Toss well to combine. Transfer the shrimp to a large serving bowl or platter, and serve immediately.

JOHNNY VINCZENCZ
SIMPLE BARBECUED CHICKEN TACO WITH BACKYARD MANGO SALSA <small>kid friendly</small>

This dish was created for a kids' cooking class at SoBe in 2009. The goal was something healthy, fun, and easy, to let the little ones test their culinary chops without losing fingers! They all seemed to enjoy the class, and I only had to duck once or twice to escape the flying avocado. The combination of barbecue, mango, and avocado is fresh and zesty and very South Florida. The mangos literally came from my backyard; different mangos ripen at different times and so we're lucky enough to get them from early summer into late fall. Half my staff has some kind of mango tree at home. We use as many as we can, then peel and clean the rest, saving them for purees and sorbet.

SERVES 4

4 boneless, skinless chicken breasts

6 tablespoons favorite barbecue sauce, plus more for serving

1 large mango, peeled, pitted, and cut into small dice

2 tablespoons small-diced red onion

2 tablespoons small-diced green bell pepper

12 fresh cilantro leaves, chopped, plus more for garnish

Juice of 1 lime

2 tablespoons olive oil

Salt and freshly ground black pepper

4 fresh white corn tortillas

Vegetable oil, for tortillas

6 tablespoons shredded lettuce

8 slices avocado

1. In a baking dish, marinate the chicken breasts in the barbecue sauce. Cover and refrigerate for 1 hour.

2. Heat a grill to medium-high.

3. Remove the chicken from the sauce and grill until completely cooked, about 4 minutes on each side, depending on thickness. Set aside at room temperature.

4. In a bowl, combine the mango, onion, bell pepper, cilantro, lime juice, and olive oil. Season with salt and pepper and set aside.

5. Warm a nonstick pan or griddle. Lightly rub both sides of a tortilla with vegetable oil. Place the tortilla in the pan and heat until lightly browned, 1 minute on each side. Do not let the tortilla get crisp. Repeat with the remaining tortillas. Set aside.

6. Cut the warm chicken into thin strips. Lay the tortillas on a clean surface, and top each one with some lettuce, chicken, mango salsa, and 2 slices of avocado. Quickly fold the tortillas and place them on plates. Drizzle each tortilla with some barbecue sauce and sprinkle with cilantro.

CHRIS LILLY
BUBBLEQ PULLED PORK

After cooking whole pork shoulders in South Beach for so many years, it became a tradition to have a "Puttin' on the Pork Party" the night before the BubbleQ. Everyone in the know would show up at the beach at midnight to prep the pork shoulders, listen to music, and celebrate! In 2008, I was given pork butts instead of whole pork shoulders to cook. This cut is the upper portion of the pork shoulder and about half the size, which means half the cook-time. So when I arrived at the beach at sunrise to begin cooking, I was greeted with a throng of people who had started the party without me six hours earlier! Remember, part of the fun of barbecuing is how you spend your time while the meat is on the grill, not just the end result. So when cooking this at home, have plenty of family and friends around to share the good times and celebrate.

SERVES 10 TO 12

INJECTION

⅓ cup apple juice

⅓ cup white grape juice

¼ cup sugar

1½ tablespoons salt

PORK

1 6- to 8-pound pork butt

DRY RUB

2 teaspoons seasoned salt

1 teaspoon dark brown sugar

¾ teaspoon granulated sugar

¾ teaspoon sweet paprika

⅛ teaspoon garlic powder

⅛ teaspoon freshly ground black pepper

1/16 teaspoon mustard powder

1/16 teaspoon ground cumin

Pinch of ground ginger

SAUCE

Big Bob Gibson Bar-B-Q Championship Red Sauce (available in grocery stores in the Southeast or at BigBobGibson.com) or your favorite barbecue sauce

1. In a medium bowl, combine all the injection ingredients and mix well. Place in an injector and evenly inject the pork butt with the solution.

2. In a separate bowl, combine all the dry rub ingredients and mix well. Coat the pork butt with the dry rub, patting gently until the mixture adheres to the meat.

3. Build a fire in a grill, using wood or a combination of charcoal and wood for indirect cooking. Heat the grill to 250°F.

SOBE SNAPSHOTS: CHEF CHRIS LILLY

"The day after the BubbleQ in 2006, I went deep-sea fishing with my great friend Adam Perry Lang, chef/owner of Daisy May's BBQ in New York City. Our catch included three beautiful mahimahi, and on our way back to South Beach, we planned a fish barbecue for the next day. My BBQ trailer—I tow it down from Decatur, Alabama, behind a truck—was tucked away in an alley just south of the Royal Palm Hotel and I knew it could handle slow-smoking the fish, along with grilling potatoes, veggies, and corn on the cob. We invited everyone we knew in Miami and also fed the lucky ones who just happened down that alley . . . perhaps thirty or thirty-five people total. Fresh mojitos were aplenty and a commemorative bottle of Moët was uncorked. And Margaret Braun showed up with the crown jewel: the top layer of the cake she had baked for the SoBe Fifth Anniversary party the night before. What we were doing *certainly* couldn't have been legal: firing up two giant charcoal-and-wood rotisserie cookers on a canopied nineteen-foot trailer in an alley between two Miami Beach hotels! But looking at our buffet, we knew we had plenty of bribes to offer if we needed them! We skinned one side of the mahi, used a wet rub, started with a low-temperature smoke, and then finished hot. The fish turned out great! It was truly a perfect ending to yet another perfect SoBe weekend."

4. Place the pork butt on the grill, away from the fire, and cook with the grill cover on for 7 to 9 hours. Add hot charcoal or wood coals as needed during the cooking process to keep the grill temperature stable. The internal temperature of the meat should reach 190°F.

5. Remove from the heat. Slice, pull, or chop the meat. Drizzle with the sauce, and serve.

ELIZABETH A. KARMEL
TEXAS HILL COUNTRY BRISKET

Barbecue doesn't come any purer than what they serve in the Hill Country and central Texas. The rub they love there is simply salt, coarse-ground black pepper, and cayenne, while the meat is flavored by the sweet smoke of post oak. That part of Texas is a "no sauce" zone where folks savor unadorned meat: rich and beefy, a little bit salty, tinged a rosy pink from the smoke. This recipe for brisket is as close to authentic Texas barbecue as you can get outside of the Lone Star State!

SERVES 8 TO 20, DEPENDING ON APPETITE

1 7- to 9-pound whole beef brisket, untrimmed

½ cup Lockhart Dry Rub (recipe follows)

1 bottle beer (try Lone Star or a Shiner Bock for a Texas flair)

Post oak or oak wood chips, soaked in water for 30 minutes

Cucumber salad and/or pickled okra, avocado slices, jalapeños, sliced white onion, Longhorn cheddar cheese, saltine crackers, sliced white bread

1. Sprinkle the brisket liberally with the rub.

2. Set up a charcoal grill for indirect cooking, or place a smoker box in a gas grill. Pour the beer into a drip pan and place the pan on the charcoal grate between the two piles of briquettes. If using a gas grill, pour the beer into a small drip pan and put it in the far left corner of the cooking grates. (The beer is in the pan to add moisture to the cooking environment while the meat smokes. This is a good idea any time you smoke-cook foods for a long period of time because smoke reduces the moisture in the air.)

3. Place the wood chips directly on the gray-ashed briquettes, if using charcoal, or in the smoker box in your gas grill.

4. Place the brisket, fat side up, in the center of the cooking grate over the drip pan. You will not turn the brisket during the cooking time at all. Grill for 5 to 7 hours, or until a meat thermometer registers 180°F. (If using charcoal, be sure to add fresh briquettes each hour to keep the heat constant.) When it is done, remove the brisket from the grill and let it rest for 20 minutes.

5. Slice the meat thin and serve with a cucumber salad and/or the assorted accoutrements.

LOCKHART DRY RUB

MAKES ¾ CUP

½ cup Morton kosher salt

3 tablespoons coarsely ground black pepper

2 teaspoons cayenne pepper

Combine the salt, black pepper, and cayenne in a bowl and mix well. Store in an airtight container.

"ORGANIZING HUGE EVENTS FEATURING SEVERAL CHEFS IS AN ART, AND THE BUBBLEQ SETS THE GOLD STANDARD. NOT ONLY DO WE LOVE TO HANG OUT WITH OUR BUDS, WE GET TO WORK WITH TERRIFIC STUDENTS AND GET A GLIMPSE OF THE NEXT GENERATION OF CULINARY CHAMPS."

—MARY SUE MILLIKEN AND SUSAN FENIGER

RICK BAYLESS
BRAVA STEAK WITH LAZY SALSA

I chose this dish for one of my SoBe demos because it shows an easy grilling technique. In almost twenty-five years, we've never taken it off the Frontera Grill menu—our guests keep asking for it. In the summer months, we grow a "salsa garden" on our rooftop in downtown Chicago. Our chefs harvest chiles, herbs, and tomatoes every day and make a rooftop salsa to accompany the steak. There really isn't anything else like it!

SERVES 6

MARINADE

6 large cloves garlic (unpeeled)

4 fresh serrano or 2 jalapeño chiles, stemmed

¼ cup freshly squeezed lime juice

2 tablespoons vegetable or olive oil, plus more for steaks

Salt

6 1-inch-thick ribeye steaks (10 to 12 ounces each)

Vegetable or olive oil

Lazy Salsa (recipe follows) or another salsa or hot sauce of your liking

FOR THE MARINADE

1. In a small ungreased skillet set over medium heat, roast the garlic and the chiles, turning them occasionally, until both are soft and blotchy black in places: 5 to 10 minutes for the chiles and 10 to 15 minutes for the garlic. Remove from the heat and let cool; then peel the garlic. Place the garlic and chiles in a food processor, and add the lime juice and oil. Run the machine until the mixture is as smoothly pureed as possible. Season it highly with salt, usually about 1½ teaspoons.

2. Smear the marinade over both sides of the steaks, cover, and refrigerate for 1 hour.

TO GRILL THE STEAKS

1. Light a charcoal fire and let the coals burn until they are covered with gray ash. Position the grill grate and let it heat for about 2 minutes.

2. Remove the steaks from the marinade, and spray or brush them on both sides with a little oil. Place on the grill grates and cook for 3 to 4 minutes, or until the grates have nicely

recipe continues

seared beautiful grill marks into the meat. (Don't attempt to move the steaks until you can see grill marks.) Flip the steaks and cook until they are as done as you like, typically 2 to 3 minutes longer for medium-rare. I like to let the steaks rest for a few minutes (on a cool part of the grill, on a grate suspended over the back of the grill, or in a very-low-temperature oven) before serving to allow the meat to reabsorb all the juices.

3. Serve with Lazy Salsa.

LAZY SALSA

MAKES 2½ CUPS; SERVES 6

4 medium-small red-ripe round tomatoes (about 1½ pounds)

1 medium onion, cut in half

3 or 4 jalapeños, stemmed

4 cloves garlic (unpeeled)

Salt

1. Light a charcoal fire and let the coals burn until they are covered with gray ash. Position the grill grate and let it heat for 2 minutes.

2. Place the tomatoes, onion, jalapeños, and garlic on the grill (see Note). Grill the vegetables, turning them occasionally, until they are well charred: about 10 minutes for the garlic, 15 minutes for the chiles, and 20 minutes for the tomatoes and onion. Remove the ingredients as they are done and place them on a rimmed baking sheet. Let cool. Peel the garlic. If you wish, you can pull the charred skins off the tomatoes.

3. Combine the chiles and garlic in a food processor, and pulse until coarsely pureed. Add the tomatoes and any juices that have collected on the baking sheet, and pulse until roughly chopped.

4. Chop the onion and place it in a bowl. Stir in the tomato mixture, along with about 2 tablespoons water, or enough to give the salsa an easily spoonable consistency. Taste and season with salt, usually about 1 teaspoon.

Note: To keep the garlic from dropping through and to make cleanup easy, I typically place a perforated grill pan on the grates, heat it up, then lay the vegetables on it.

DEAN FEARING
BARBECUE SHRIMP TACO WITH MANGO–PICKLED RED ONION SALAD

This taco is now the signature item at Fearing's Restaurant in Dallas. After serving it at the BubbleQ in 2006, I knew it would be a hit because of the three main ingredients that really say "Texas"—barbecue, lime, and cilantro. To me, anything wrapped in a flour tortilla is absolutely delicious.

SERVES 4

½ tablespoon vegetable oil

1 cup small-diced peeled and deveined shrimp

Salt and freshly cracked black pepper

1 cup diced onion

1 cup barbecue sauce

½ cup grated jalapeño Jack cheese

4 6-inch flour tortillas, cooked and kept warm

Mango–Pickled Red Onion Salad (recipe follows)

⅓ cup grated Cotija or Mexican farmer's cheese

⅓ cup toasted and coarsely ground Mexican pumpkin seeds

4 fresh serrano chiles

4 sprigs fresh cilantro

1. Heat the oil in a large sauté pan set over medium heat. Add the shrimp to the hot pan and season with salt and pepper. Sauté for 1 minute, or until the shrimp turns red. Add the onion and sauté for 2 minutes, or until translucent. Stir in the barbecue sauce. Bring to a boil and quickly remove the pan from the heat. Add the Jack cheese and stir until the cheese has melted into the mixture.

2. Place a warm tortilla in the middle of each warm serving plate. Spoon equal portions of the shrimp mixture into the middle of each tortilla. Roll each tortilla into a cylinder with the seam side down. Spoon a small portion of Mango–Pickled Red Onion Salad on top of each taco. Sprinkle with the Cotija cheese and pumpkin seeds, and garnish with the chiles (to be eaten like a pickle by the adventurous) and cilantro.

recipe continues

"I LOVE THAT MOMENT AT THE BUBBLEQ JUST BEFORE THE GATES OPEN. ALL THE CHEFS ARE GETTING READY AT THEIR INDIVIDUAL STATIONS AND IT'S THE CALM BEFORE THE STORM, BEFORE THOUSANDS OF PEOPLE COME FLOODING THROUGH."

—DEAN FEARING

MANGO–PICKLED RED ONION SALAD

MAKES ABOUT 4 CUPS

PICKLED RED ONIONS

1 red onion

½ cup white wine vinegar

½ cup sugar

Pinch of salt

CUMIN-LIME VINAIGRETTE

½ cup olive oil

½ cup vegetable oil

½ cup freshly squeezed lime juice

1 small onion, cut into small dice

1 cup freshly squeezed orange juice

3 tablespoons maple syrup

2 tablespoons malt vinegar

½ tablespoon whole cumin seeds, toasted

Salt

3 cups julienned green cabbage

2 ripe mangos, peeled, pitted, and cut into julienne

1 cup small-diced jicama

½ cup pecans, toasted

¼ cup finely sliced cilantro leaves

Salt

FOR THE PICKLED RED ONIONS

1. Cut the onion in half and then slice it into very thin half-moon shapes. Place them in a small heatproof bowl and set aside.

2. In a small saucepan set over medium heat, heat the vinegar and sugar, stirring constantly. When the sugar has dissolved, remove from the heat. Add the salt and pour the mixture over the onions. Cover with plastic wrap, place in the refrigerator, and allow to pickle for 8 to 12 hours.

FOR THE VINAIGRETTE

1. Combine the oils and the lime juice in a medium bowl and set aside.

2. In a small saucepan, bring the onion, orange juice, maple syrup, vinegar, and cumin seeds to a boil. Cook for about 5 minutes, or until the mixture has reduced to almost dry. Remove from the heat and place in a blender. Puree until smooth. Add to the lime juice mixture. Season with salt, and stir until completely blended.

TO MAKE THE SALAD

1. Drain the pickled onions.

2. In a medium bowl, combine the cabbage, mangos, onions, jicama, pecans, and cilantro. Slowly add the vinaigrette, tossing until the salad is lightly coated. Season with salt to taste, and use immediately.

ROBERT DEL GRANDE
BEER-MOPPED RIBEYE STEAKS WITH BACON, ONIONS, AND GARLIC

Years ago I prepared a dish similar to this one at SoBe and found that nothing attracts a crowd faster than forty or fifty double-thick ribeyes all grilling at once. Where there's smoke, there's fire, and where there's fire, there are steaks. And there was me with a big basting brush, slathering those big ribeyes with this beer mop. I sliced those steaks all night and I thought the line of people would never end! Now when I cook this dish at home, I always think about that time at SoBe and how two steaks are a whole lot easier than fifty! I like to serve these with roasted fingerling potatoes and a big red wine.

SERVES 4

BEER MOP

1 12-ounce bottle dark beer

¼ cup (packed) brown sugar (dark or light)

2 tablespoons ancho chile powder

2 tablespoons paprika (sweet or hot)

½ cup peanut oil or light extra-virgin olive oil

2 tablespoons red wine vinegar

2 chipotle chiles (canned in adobo)

2 tablespoons adobo (from canned chiles)

1 teaspoon salt

½ teaspoon freshly ground black pepper

BACON, ONIONS, AND GARLIC

1 tablespoon extra-virgin olive oil

2 slices bacon, cut into small pieces

1 large or 2 small white onions, cut into ½-inch pieces

4 cloves garlic, chopped

½ teaspoon salt

¼ teaspoon freshly ground black pepper

2 16-ounce ribeye steaks

1 jalapeño, cut into very thin rounds

½ cup (loosely packed) flat-leaf parsley leaves

FOR THE BEER MOP

Bring the beer to a boil in a large saucepan, and reduce it to ½ cup. Remove from the heat. Add the brown sugar, chile powder, and paprika and stir. Transfer the mixture to a blender. Add the peanut oil, vinegar, chiles, adobo, salt, and pepper, and puree until smooth. Set aside.

FOR THE BACON, ONIONS, AND GARLIC

Heat the olive oil in a broad skillet. Add the bacon and lightly sauté. Add the onions and garlic, and sauté until lightly golden brown. Season with the salt and pepper, and remove from the heat.

FOR THE RIBEYE STEAKS

1. Prepare a hot charcoal fire to one side of a grill. Brush the steaks with the beer mop. Grill over the charcoal fire for 6 to 8 minutes per side for medium-rare, basting occasionally to generate a caramelized and mahogany-colored look. Move the steaks to the side of the grill without charcoal and allow them to rest.

2. Reheat the bacon-onion mixture until very hot. Add the jalapeño and parsley.

3. Remove the steaks from the grill and cut them crosswise into ¼-inch-thick slices. Arrange the slices on a platter, and spoon the bacon-onion mixture over the steak. Drizzle with some olive oil, and serve.

"IF LEE WERE TO RESIGN? I'D BREAK HIS NECK AND DRAG HIM BACK HERE."

—MEL DICK, PARTNER AND PRESIDENT OF THE WINE DIVISION,

SOUTHERN WINE & SPIRITS

KENT RATHBUN

WOOD-GRILLED PORK TENDERLOIN WITH PEACH BARBECUE SAUCE AND BOURBON CREAM CORN

The smokiness of this pork tenderloin combined with the natural sweet taste of peaches just screams summer barbecue. At our restaurants we use a combination of hickory and oak wood. At home, the aroma of mesquite would definitely make your neighbors come running.

SERVES 8

PEACH BARBECUE SAUCE

8 ounces smoked bacon, diced (1 ham hock may be substituted)

1 cup coarsely chopped smoked or grilled onion

4 cloves smoked or grilled garlic, chopped

2 árbol chiles, stems removed

2 cups coarsely chopped fresh or dried peaches

1 tablespoon freshly cracked black pepper

2 tablespoons Worcestershire sauce

2 cups freshly squeezed orange juice

2 cups ketchup

6 dashes Tabasco sauce

Juice of 2 lemons

2 teaspoons kosher salt

PORK TENDERLOINS

8 8-ounce pieces pork tenderloin, trimmed of fat and silverskin

6 tablespoons olive oil

2 tablespoons kosher salt

2 tablespoons freshly cracked black pepper

1 tablespoon granulated garlic

Bourbon Cream Corn (recipe follows)

Crispy Fried Onions, for garnish (recipe follows)

FOR THE PEACH BARBECUE SAUCE

1. In a small saucepan set over medium heat, cook the bacon until crisp. Then add the onion and garlic and sauté until caramelized.

2. Add the chiles and continue to cook until they start to toast. Add the peaches and the pepper. Deglaze the pan with the Worcestershire sauce and orange juice.

3. Reduce the juice until it has started to thicken. Add the ketchup and reduce the heat to low. Continue cooking for about 15 minutes.

4. Add the Tabasco, lemon juice, and salt. Remove from the heat. Strain the barbecue sauce and set it aside.

recipe continues

FOR THE PORK TENDERLOINS

If you're using aromatic woods on your outdoor grill, use logs or chips. No need to soak them.

1. Heat a grill or broiler to high. On a baking sheet, rub the tenderloins with the oil. Season them with the salt, pepper, and granulated garlic.

2. Grill over an open flame or on a charbroiler until the desired doneness is reached, 3½ to 4 minutes per all sides for medium-rare.

3. Remove the meat from the grill or broiler and slice each tenderloin. Serve with Bourbon Cream Corn and finish with the Peach Barbecue Sauce. Garnish with Crispy Fried Onions.

BOURBON CREAM CORN

SERVES 8

4 tablespoons butter

4 shallots, minced

4 cloves garlic, minced

3 cups fresh corn kernels

4 tablespoons diced red bell pepper

4 tablespoons bourbon

1 cup heavy cream

¼ cup chopped scallions, white and tender green parts

1 tablespoon freshly cracked black pepper

1 tablespoon kosher salt

1. Heat the butter in a large sauté pan. Add the shallots and garlic, and sauté until translucent, about 1 minute. Add the corn and bell peppers, and continue cooking for 2 minutes.

2. Deglaze the pan with the bourbon, and add the cream. Bring the cream to a boil and reduce for 2 to 3 minutes. The cream will start to thicken. Finish with the scallions, black pepper, and salt.

CRISPY FRIED ONIONS

1 large onion

½ cup all-purpose flour

Cayenne pepper

Kosher salt

Canola oil

1. Slice the onion into extremely thin slices. Season the flour with the cayenne and salt to taste, and toss the onion slices in the seasoned flour.

2. Heat the oil to 350°F. Fry the onion slices until crisp, about 2 minutes. Use immediately.

STEVEN RAICHLEN
CAVEMAN RIB STEAK WITH EMBER-CHARRED PEPPER SAUCE

I created the Caveman Rib Steak for the first SoBe festival in 2002, when Lee asked me to organize the BubbleQ. One of our pit masters roasted whole salmons in front of a bonfire, the way the Pacific Northwest Indians have done for millennia, and that's the inspiration for this ember-roasted rib steak. Grilling in the embers gives the meat a smoky crust that you just can't duplicate on a conventional grill. Add a topping of fried garlic, peppers, and cilantro, and you get a steak that explodes with flavor. To be strictly authentic, use a charcoal grill. If you don't have one, heat a dry cast-iron skillet to screaming hot on a gas grill and cook the steak (lightly brushed with olive oil) in it. A porterhouse could be "grilled" the same way.

SERVES 2 TO 3

1 1½- to 2-inch-thick bone-in rib steak
(1½ to 2 pounds)

Coarse salt or rock salt

Cracked black pepper

PEPPER SAUCE

5 tablespoons extra-virgin olive oil

1 red or yellow bell pepper, cut into
1 x ¼-inch strips

5 cloves garlic, thinly sliced

¼ cup coarsely chopped fresh cilantro

1. Build a charcoal fire. When the coals glow orange, rake them into an even layer. Fan the coals with a newspaper or bellows to blow off any loose ash.

2. Generously, and I mean generously, season the steak on both sides with salt and cracked pepper. Place the steak directly on the embers. Grill, turning it with long-handled tongs, until it is darkly browned or even charred on the outside and cooked to taste inside: 4 to 6 minutes per side for medium-rare.

3. Using the tongs, lift the steak out of the fire, shaking it to dislodge any embers. Using a basting brush, brush off any loose ash. Arrange the steak on a heatproof platter. Let the steak rest, loosely tented with foil, while you make the sauce.

4. Heat the oil in a cast-iron skillet placed directly on the embers, on the side burners of a gas grill, or on the stove. When the oil is hot, add the bell peppers, garlic, and cilantro. Cook over high heat for about 2 minutes, or until the sauce is aromatic and the peppers and garlic are lightly browned. Immediately pour the sauce over the steak and serve at once.

KENNY CALLAGHAN
BABY BACK RIBS

This recipe highlights the pork's natural flavor, creating a really juicy, flavorful rib. It's also very simple and calls for ingredients most home chefs readily have in their spice rack—which is why I often make this rub when I'm on vacation with my family or cooking for friends at home.

SERVES 6

BABY BACK BBQ SAUCE

½ cup diced onion

2 tablespoons vegetable oil

1 tablespoon finely chopped garlic

1 teaspoon sweet paprika

1 teaspoon chili powder

1 teaspoon freshly ground black pepper

1 teaspoon ground cumin

½ teaspoon ground coriander

½ teaspoon cayenne pepper

½ teaspoon celery salt

½ teaspoon kosher salt

1½ cups ketchup

2 tablespoons honey

2 tablespoons dark molasses

2 tablespoons dark brown sugar

2 tablespoons Worcestershire sauce

1 tablespoon apple cider vinegar

3 racks baby back ribs

Baby Back Rib Rub (recipe follows)

FOR THE BARBECUE SAUCE

1. In a medium stainless-steel saucepan over medium heat, sauté the onions in the oil for 5 minutes, or until they are translucent.

2. Add the garlic to the pan and sauté for 2 minutes more.

3. Add the paprika, chili powder, black pepper, cumin, coriander, cayenne, celery salt, and kosher salt. Toast the spices but do not let them burn, roughly 2 to 3 minutes.

4. Add the ketchup, honey, molasses, brown sugar, Worcestershire sauce, and vinegar, and bring the sauce to a boil. Remove from the heat and strain the sauce to remove the onions. Cool the sauce in the refrigerator.

FOR THE RIBS

1. Remove the membrane from the underside of the rack of ribs. Liberally season the ribs on both sides with the rub until the entire rack is evenly coated. Cover and refrigerate the ribs for 18 to 24 hours.

2. Heat a smoker or an oven to 210°F.

recipe continues

3. Remove the ribs from the refrigerator and cook for 5½ to 6 hours, or until tender. In the last 5 minutes of the cooking process, liberally baste the ribs with the barbecue sauce. Serve immediately.

BABY BACK RIB RUB

MAKES ABOUT ⅓ CUP

1 tablespoon plus ½ teaspoon granulated sugar

1 teaspoon (packed) dark brown sugar

1½ teaspoons granulated garlic

1½ teaspoons ground cumin

1½ teaspoons celery salt

1½ teaspoons ground fennel

1½ teaspoons chili powder

1 teaspoon granulated onion

1 teaspoon ground coriander

½ teaspoon cayenne pepper

½ teaspoon Spanish paprika

½ teaspoon freshly ground black pepper

½ teaspoon freshly ground white pepper

½ teaspoon kosher salt

¼ teaspoon ground celery seeds

Combine all the ingredients in a bowl, and stir well to mix evenly.

"LIKE MANY OF LEE'S IDEAS, BARBECUE AND CHAMPAGNE SEEMED A LITTLE OFF-THE-WALL. BUT IT WAS EXPLOSIVELY POPULAR, AND TEN YEARS LATER, IT'S STILL THE HARDEST TICKET TO GET."

—RICHARD BOOTH, VICE PRESIDENT/GENERAL MANAGER,

SOUTHERN WINE & SPIRITS, SOUTH FLORIDA

ADAM PERRY LANG
BRINED SHRIMP GRILLED IN THEIR SHELLS WITH SCOTCH BONNET DRIZZLE

Here's a fun, clean South Beach dish that I created for the BubbleQ in 2009. It's nice as an appetizer or as a main course for lunch. Grilling in the shells intensifies the shrimp's flavors, while protecting them from the intensity of harsh heat. These babies are moist, plump, and delicious, and the Scotch bonnet adds a hot fruity kick, mellowed somewhat by the sugar. Serve them with sliced sweet ripe mango and a peppery arugula salad: hot, sweet, and spicy make a great hot-weather combination.

SERVES 8

BRINE

8 cups water

¼ cup kosher salt

2 tablespoons sugar

Juice of 2 lemons

8 cloves garlic, grated on a Microplane

3 cups ice cubes

24 jumbo shrimp, shells on, back split and vein removed

HOT PEPPER DRIZZLE

1 cup water

⅓ cup canola or vegetable oil

½ cup sugar

Juice of 1 lime

3 Scotch bonnet or habañero chiles, seeds removed, chopped (careful—these peppers are extremely hot)

Canola or vegetable oil, for brushing

Dressing (recipe follows)

FOR THE BRINE

In a large bowl, combine the water, salt, sugar, lemon juice, and garlic. Add the ice and mix well. Add the shrimp and let brine in the refrigerator or at room temperature for 1 hour.

FOR THE HOT PEPPER DRIZZLE

Combine the water, oil, sugar, lime juice, and chiles in a small saucepan, and bring to a boil. Simmer for 10 minutes. Remove from the heat and puree with a hand blender. Set aside.

recipe continues

TO COOK THE SHRIMP

1. Heat a grill to medium.

2. Drain the shrimp; discard the brine. Brush the shrimp with some oil. Grill over direct heat for about 5 minutes on each side.

3. Remove the shrimp from the grill and immediately place them in a bowl with the dressing. Toss, place on a platter, and drizzle to your heat tolerance with the Hot Pepper Drizzle.

DRESSING

MAKES ABOUT 1¼ CUPS

½ cup extra-virgin olive oil

¼ cup fresh cilantro leaves

¼ cup finely chopped red bell pepper

¼ cup chopped scallions, white and tender green parts

Juice of 2 lemons

Grated zest of 1 lemon

2 tablespoons minced fresh chives

Kosher salt and freshly ground black pepper

In a bowl, combine the oil, cilantro, bell pepper, scallions, lemon juice, zest, and chives. Season with salt and pepper to taste, and set aside.

"THE SMELL OF A CHICKEN ON AN OPEN FIRE WAS MY FIRST FOOD MEMORY, THE SMELL OF THE FAT DRIPPING ON THE FIRE, THE GATHERING OF FRIENDS AND FAMILY . . . THAT'S WHAT A BARBECUE IS ALL ABOUT! ALL CULTURES AND COUNTRIES HAVE A VERSION OF COOKING ON AN OPEN FIRE. AND AT THE BUBBLEQ, WE CAN TASTE MOST OF THEM!

—HUNG HUYNH

MING TSAI
SWORDFISH-BACON KEBABS WITH CILANTRO GREMOLATA

I'm probably one of the few people in Massachusetts who grills year-round—I just love the smoky, intense flavors. I demoed this simple dish at SoBe in 2008 and it's still one of my favorites. As much as I like ribs and burgers, you can't live on that alone. So when I crave something lighter that still has the heft of meat, I reach for swordfish, which is substantial and especially well suited to grilling. The bacon adds texture, but you could easily skip it. The gremolata is my East/West take on the classic Italian combination. I love dipping sauces, and so do my kids—they make eating that much more fun. This is a dish you can serve as an appetizer or entrée: simple enough to make every night but special enough for company . . . my idea of the perfect recipe!

SERVES 4

Nonstick cooking spray

GREMOLATA

1 cup chopped fresh cilantro

3 lemons, zested and juiced

1 tablespoon minced garlic

2 stalks lemongrass (white parts only), finely minced

½ cup extra-virgin olive oil

Kosher salt and freshly ground black pepper

KEBABS

4 8-inch-long satay skewers, soaked in water

12 slices bacon

1½ pounds center-cut swordfish, cut into 1-inch cubes

1 pint cherry tomatoes

Kosher salt and freshly ground black pepper

Prepare a hot grill, sprayed slick with cooking spray.

FOR THE GREMOLATA

In a bowl, combine the cilantro, lemon zest and juice, garlic, lemongrass, and oil. Season with salt and pepper.

FOR THE KEBABS

1. Assemble the kebabs by first skewering one end of a bacon slice and following with a swordfish cube. Weave the bacon in between the swordfish and tomatoes as you thread

each onto the skewer. Lay the kebabs in a baking dish, and rub a third of the gremolata all over the kebabs. Let marinate for at least 20 minutes.

2. Season the kebabs with kosher salt and pepper and grill for about 8 minutes, or until the bacon is cooked through.

3. Arrange 1 skewer on each plate (satay plates if you have them), and serve with the remaining gremolata in a dipping bowl.

CHAPTER 4
BURGERS

When Rachael Ray and I decided to celebrate the country's best burgers by creating the Burger Bash, we couldn't have imagined how right our timing would be. Since the first Bash was held at SoBe in 2007, burgers have exploded in popularity. The bash was a total no-brainer. Who doesn't love a great burger?

I grew up eating at Friendly's on Long Island, where they had terrific patty melts. And whenever I see one on a menu today, I never fail to order it. But really, any kind of burger will do. I've been known to take a $40 cab ride from Manhattan to Brooklyn to have a $4 burger!

And Rachael shares my obsession. Her passion for burgers always makes this one of our most anticipated, most publicized events—and always among the very first to sell out. (Started in 2007, our New York City Wine & Food Festival has a wildly popular Burger Bash as well.)

Burgers may be casual in real life, but here at the Burger Bash, they're serious business. The chefs who are invited to cook go all out, topping and stuffing their prized patties with everything from wild-boar bacon to truffles and foie gras. The burgers served at SoBe have some of the finest pedigrees around.

Take Daniel Boulud's DB Burger, made famous at his DB Bistro Moderne in Manhattan: sirloin filled with braised short ribs, black truffle, and foie gras, topped with fresh horseradish mayo and fresh and confit tomato, served in a toasted Parmesan bun.

"Daniel is a giant in the industry," says Burger Bash event manager Randy Fisher, "and he never gives less than his best. Making eight hundred burgers for us, he could have pulled back on the foie gras—used a substitute or smaller portions. But Daniel totally delivered."

Even the simplest burger gets the royal treatment at SoBe. Most chefs work with prime meat from Allen Brothers, an event sponsor, which donates the product and blends it to each chef's exacting specs. Typically the chefs request an 80/20 (chuck and sirloin) blend, but some add short ribs to the mix. One chef even requested a combo of chuck, sirloin, brisket, and short ribs!

To feed a crowd of 2,000 or so at the Burger Bash, roughly two dozen chefs are asked to prepare about 800 portions each. Some serve 800 full-size burgers, while

others prepare 800 and then cut them into quarters. Some do elegant little sliders that fit neatly in the palm of your hand.

Creativity runs high. One year chef Thomas Connell did burgers in tempura batter, and another year, burgers in empanadas. The crowd went crazy the year that Henry Meer wrapped a burger in a potato knish. Rick Bayless mixed homemade Mexican-style chorizo into his burger meat one year, while Jeremy Fox did a vegan "boudin noir" made with black Italian rice.

Pretzel buns, brioche buns, griddled muffins, English muffins . . . we think we've seen it all. Then each year something new comes in and blows us all away. "I love seeing some of the fanciest chefs in the business all serious out there flipping burgers!" Rachael says.

When it comes to thinking outside the bun, our chefs shine there too: sides served at the Burger Bash are anything but mundane. In fact, the go-withs at SoBe are every bit as important as the burgers.

Would you like Lobster Potato Fritters and Lime Habañero Aioli with that?

The morning of the Burger Bash, the out-of-town chefs start showing up for prep in the banquet kitchens of the Ritz-Carlton, South Beach, sometime around 9:00. Some even come in the day before. (Local chefs use their own kitchens.) Waiting for the chefs are their pre-ordered ingredients so they can get right to work. Later, their ready-to-grill burgers and side dishes are transported to the massive tent on the beach, where each chef mans his or her own kitchen station. In the weeks prior to the Bash, the chefs will have told Randy, the event manager, exactly what they'll need: grills (flat-top, gas, or charcoal), ovens, fryers, coolers, blenders, small wares, and more.

You know it's party time when the wonderful smell of sizzling burgers begins drifting down the beach. Guests start milling around the entryway more than an hour before the party starts, while inside the tent the chefs have already started grilling and griddling to juicy perfection. There's also icy cold Amstel Light beer, plenty of great wine, desserts, live music, and more.

"SoBe takes America's favorite sandwich and lets chefs just go wild on it," says Bobby Flay, a loyal festival veteran who cooks at SoBe events each year, "and then serve it by the ocean with beautiful weather in February. I mean, really, what else do you need?"

A panel of industry judges decides who wins best topping, side dish, and so forth, while party guests cast votes for the prestigious People's Choice Award. Followed by a flock of reporters and TV cameras, I escort Rachael and her husband, John, around the tent to taste every burger and chat up the chefs. Then Rachael takes the stage and announces the winners to loud cheers.

Chefs want to win Burger Bash awards for the validation, bragging rights, and tons of sensational publicity. But there have been some pretty serious prizes as well, including a VIP European trip for two and a $5,000 FIU scholarship in the chef's name.

The party winds down around 10 p.m., but after an evening this magical, most people seem hesitant to leave. "Miami Beach wants us off the beach by 11 p.m.," Randy Fisher says, "and we need time to clear the venue. At 10:57 p.m., we threaten to use water cannons on the stragglers."

In 2009, a new record was set when all Burger Bash tickets were grabbed up by 9 a.m. on the first day of sales. But it's not just the paying guests who go crazy for this event: the chefs love the revelry and rivalry and the idea that it's for a great cause.

THE BEST WINES FOR BURGERS

ACCORDING TO BEST CELLARS' COFOUNDER AND WINE DIRECTOR JOSH WESSON, PAIRING WINE WITH BURGERS IS NO DIFFERENT THAN PAIRING IT WITH OTHER FOODS—IT ALL COMES DOWN TO FINDING SIMILARITIES AND/OR CONTRASTS IN THE TASTES AND TEXTURES. THAT SAID, JOSH SUGGESTS A FEW THINGS YOU CAN DO TO INCREASE YOUR CHANCES OF A GREAT MATCH.

- Best to leave the jugs and boxes closed, and open a bottle or two of something good, but not *too* good. Save your Pétrus for holier cows: Burgerville is a $20-and-under town!

- Stay away from bottles boasting alcohol levels above 14.5 percent. Such high octane will burn even hotter if it comes in contact with a mound of warm, well-seasoned meat—especially if it's draped with a slab of salty bacon and cheese.

- Even when going with a red wine, it's a good idea to chill the bottle a bit before pouring—30 minutes in the fridge will ice the deal. The slight coolness of the liquid will refresh the palate and cut through the burger's fat.

- If your burger comes topped with sweet'n'savory condiments like ketchup, barbecue sauce, or Russian dressing, choose a fruit-forward rosé or red wine, or a sweet'n'tangy white wine that echoes those tastes. Pairing "like with like" will both flatter the food and preserve the wine's flavor balance.

- Rare burgers mean juicy meat, and juicy meat doesn't require additional juiciness from the wine to bring out its best. The converse holds true for burgers that are cooked beyond medium: the more well-done the burger, the juicier the wine should be, with the wine's mouthwatering qualities serving to moisten the dry meat.

- Tannin, an astringent component in red wine, is also good for cleansing the palate of animal fat. If your slider's super-slippery, just up the tannins in your glass.

- There aren't many foods that can kill a wine—any wine—as quickly as a sour pickle. They don't call them "spears" for nothin'!

"Burger Bash is so much fun . . . I love it!" proclaims Michael Schwartz. "The super energy comes from the concept itself: casual clothes, on the beach, freshly cooked burgers, top chefs. And the students who help are just awesome."

"The Bash mixes top chefs with burger-joint chefs and somehow it really works," adds Randy Garutti of Shake Shack, which won the People's Choice Award in 2007. "It's so great to see what we all create together on the beach for one night of fun."

RACHAEL RAY
CUBANO BURGER WITH MANGO–BLACK BEAN SALSA

Over the years I've written hundreds of burger recipes, from beef burgers to veggie burgers to salmon burgers . . . you name it. When I come to Miami for SoBe, I like to add a little Latin flair to my cooking. I taught this Cubano Burger at one of the culinary demos, and a year later, Lee and I started the Burger Bash, my favorite event!! Who doesn't love tasting the best burgers from the most talented chefs from all over the country?! You're going to love this one.

SERVES 4

1⅓ pounds ground turkey breast

⅓ pound deli-sliced smoked ham, chopped

2 cloves garlic, minced

¼ red bell pepper, finely chopped

3 scallions, white and tender green parts, finely chopped

2 tablespoons finely chopped fresh cilantro

1 tablespoon grill seasoning, such as McCormick's steak seasoning

Vegetable or olive oil, for drizzling

8 slices (⅓ pound) deli Swiss cheese

4 Portuguese or kaiser rolls, split

2 large dill pickles, thinly sliced lengthwise

Sliced banana pepper rings, drained

Yellow mustard

1 12-ounce bag plantain chips, such as Goya, for serving

Mango–Black Bean Salsa (recipe follows)

1. In a mixing bowl, combine the turkey, ham, garlic, bell pepper, scallions, cilantro, and seasoning. Form the mixture into 4 patties. Drizzle each patty with some oil.

2. Heat a large nonstick skillet over medium-high heat. Add the patties and cook until done (5 to 6 minutes on each side), topping each patty with 2 slices of the cheese in the last 2 minutes of the cooking time.

3. Remove from the heat and place a patty on the bottom half of each roll. Top each with some pickles and banana peppers. Slather some mustard over the inside of the top half of each roll and place it on the burger.

4. Serve with plantain chips on the side. Pass the salsa for dipping the plantains or topping the burgers.

recipe continues

MANGO–BLACK BEAN SALSA

MAKES 4 CUPS

1 16-ounce jar black bean salsa

1 ripe mango, pitted, peeled, and diced

2 tablespoons chopped fresh cilantro leaves

¼ red bell pepper, finely chopped

Place the salsa in a medium bowl, and top with the mango, cilantro, and bell pepper.

GRILLED FOR ONE MINUTE
DEVIN PADGETT

MANAGING DIRECTOR,
SOUTH BEACH WINE & FOOD FESTIVAL

Q: What's your best tip for first-time festivalgoers?

A: Pace yourselves! Don't flame out in the first few hours and ruin the rest of your experience. Too much wine, too much food, too much sun— they can take you out quickly. Have a plan and moderate!

Q: So where do the chefs all hang out after hours at SoBe?

A: As soon as word gets out, it changes. The Two 12 House pulls a lot of the talent in, but you have to be invited. And there are lots of impromptu suite and cabana parties, but again, mostly private. Chefs definitely like the bar called the Deuce . . . and the local Cuban dives such as Puerto Sagua and Café Versailles.

Q: And after all these years, what's your favorite SoBe ritual?

A: Emeril and I have a little tradition: I pick him up behind the Loews in my Bobcat to take him down the beach for his cooking demo segments. It's just a fun little five-minute thing . . . we do a few donuts in the sand and off we go. But one year I forgot or was double-booked or something. So Emeril figured he could just hop on any festival cart passing by and he jumped on one of those green maintenance carts by mistake. The driver was so starstruck, he took Emeril past the Grand Tasting Village and then dropped him there. *"Bye, Emeril, see you later!"* Emeril had to walk back through 5,000 people in the tents, with no security or escort and everyone clamoring at him. I felt so bad! Now we always double-check the plan and he's like, *"Dude! Promise you're coming to get me??"*

BOBBY FLAY
BOBBY BLUE BURGER CRUNCHIFIED

My all-time favorite meal is a cheeseburger, fries, and a shake. I'm such a burger freak, in fact, that I've opened a string of burger restaurants and written a burger cookbook (*Bobby Flay's Burgers, Fries & Shakes*). So when Lee asked me to go up against some of the country's best burger chefs at my first Bash in 2009, I wanted my burger to be awesome. Here's the one I served.

SERVES 4

8 ¼-inch-thick slices double-smoked bacon

1½ pounds 80% lean ground chuck or 90% lean ground turkey

2 tablespoons canola oil

Kosher salt and freshly ground black pepper

2 ounces blue cheese, crumbled

4 hamburger buns, split and toasted

Romaine lettuce, torn

Beefsteak tomatoes, sliced

Lay's potato chips

1. In a large sauté pan, cook the bacon over medium heat for about 5 minutes per side, or until golden brown and slightly crispy. Remove the bacon from the pan and place it on a paper-towel-lined plate to drain. Set aside.

2. Heat a grill to high. Divide the meat into four 6-ounce portions and loosely form them into ¾-inch-thick patties. Using your thumb, make a deep impression in the center of each patty. Brush the patties with the oil, and season both sides of each patty with salt and pepper to taste. Grill until the meat is slightly charred on both sides and cooked to the desired doneness, about 4 minutes per side for medium.

3. Scatter the cheese over the burgers, close the cover on the grill or loosely tent the patties with foil, and continue to cook until the cheese has melted slightly. Remove the burgers from the heat and place one on the bottom half of each bun. Top each hamburger with 2 slices of the bacon, some lettuce, a couple of tomato slices, and a handful of potato chips. Add the top half of the bun, and serve.

CAROL WALLACK
SOLA BURGER *NO KA OI* AND TRUFFLE FRIES

I've been working on this burger for years! *No ka oi* means "the best" in Hawaiian—and I definitely like to use the highest-quality ingredients for every component. The Cambozola cheese is a blue-vein triple-cream from Bavaria, milder than most blues, with a terrific melting quality. At my restaurant, Sola, in Chicago, we make our own bacon; it complements the caramelized onions, done in bacon fat and pineapple juice, perfectly. And the arugula is the perfect peppery accent. I love this burger on a pretzel-dough bun, but it's great on any salted-dough bun or brioche.

SERVES 4

8 slices bacon, cooked, fat reserved

6 onions, julienned

1 cup fresh pineapple juice

2 pounds wagyu (80% lean American-style kobe beef)

4 pretzel buns, split

5 ounces Cambozola cheese

16 arugula leaves

Sola Truffle Fries (recipe follows)

1. In a large skillet, sweat the onions in the reserved bacon fat over low heat. When the onions are half done, add the pineapple juice. Cook until the onions are lightly browned and sugary sweet. Remove from the heat and set aside.

2. Heat a grill to high.

3. Divide the meat into 4 portions and form them into patties. Cook until medium-rare.

4. Remove the patties from the grill and place them on the bottom halves of the buns. Divide the cheese among the burgers, then the onions and arugula. Top with the top halves of the buns. Serve with Sola Truffle Fries on the side.

recipe continues

SOLA TRUFFLE FRIES

Potato and truffle is the perfect combination. At SoBe I fried these in beef fat, but at home I'd use a canola blend. For the truffle oil spritz, I like the brand La Truffière, but Urbani is also good, although the aromas dissipate more quickly. Winning the Idaho Potato Commission Side Dish Challenge at the Burger Bash for these fries my first year at SoBe (2009) was the unexpected icing on the cake. We had such a fabulous time!

SERVES 4

Canola oil or rendered beef fat, for frying

5 Idaho russet potatoes, cut on a fry cutter and placed in water

La Truffière or Urbani white truffle oil

4 ounces freshly ground Parmigiano-Reggiano

1 tablespoon chopped fresh chives

Fine salt

1. Heat the canola oil in a deep-fat fryer until it reads 275°F.

2. Drain the potatoes and pat them very dry.

3. Add the potatoes to the fryer and blanch for 1 minute. Remove the potatoes and place them on a baking sheet to cool. Set aside.

4. Increase the oil temperature to 350°F. Return the fries to the fryer and cook until golden brown, 3 to 4 minutes. Remove the fries and place them in a mixing bowl.

5. Place some truffle oil in a spray bottle and spray the fries with the oil. Add the cheese. Sprinkle with the chives and a little salt, toss, and serve immediately.

"IT WAS SUCH AN HONOR TO BE INVITED TO 'THROWDOWN' WITH BOBBY FLAY AND THE OTHER BIG GUNS OF OUR INDUSTRY. AND SUCH A THRILL TO BRING A LITTLE VICTORY—THE BEST SIDE DISH AWARD—BACK HOME TO A NEIGHBORHOOD RESTAURANT IN CHICAGO."

—CAROL WALLACK

ART SMITH
CHEDDAR CHEESE BISCUIT BURGER WITH TOMATO GINGER CHUTNEY

I served this beauty, made with Allen Brothers Gourmet-Blend Ground Beef, at the Burger Bash in 2008. My secret weapon is the biscuits, which are always homemade just minutes before being eaten. (My motto: Have biscuits, will travel!) The tangy, spicy, sweet tomato chutney is like gourmet ketchup for grown-ups: use it to liven up burgers, chicken, pork chops, or even grilled swordfish. Enjoy the burger, but don't forget—the biscuits should be warm, delicious, and homemade!

SERVES 5

1 pound prime ground beef (the best you can find)

2 cloves garlic, minced

½ teaspoon sea salt

½ teaspoon freshly ground black pepper

5 Cheddar Cheese Biscuits (recipe follows)

Tomato-Ginger Chutney (recipe follows)

1. Heat a grill to medium-high.

2. In a large bowl, combine the beef, garlic, salt, and pepper. Form into 5 small patties. Cook to desired doneness, 3 minutes per side for medium-rare.

3. Remove the patties from the grill and place one on the bottom half of each biscuit. Top with some chutney and the top half of a biscuit.

recipe continues

CHEDDAR CHEESE BISCUITS

MAKES 12 BISCUITS

2 cups self-rising flour

2 teaspoons baking powder

1 teaspoon salt

½ teaspoon baking soda

5 tablespoons unsalted butter, chilled

½ cup grated cheddar cheese

1 cup buttermilk, plus 1 tablespoon if needed

1. Place a 10-inch cast-iron skillet in the oven and heat the oven to 425°F.

2. In a medium bowl, combine the flour, baking powder, salt, and baking soda. Cut in 4 tablespoons of the butter and ¼ cup of the cheese. Make a well in the middle of the ingredients and pour in the 1 cup buttermilk. Stir until moistened, adding an additional tablespoon of buttermilk if needed.

3. Remove the hot skillet from the oven and add the remaining 1 tablespoon butter to it. When the butter has melted, drop ¼-cup portions of the dough into the skillet, using a cookie scoop. Brush the tops of the biscuits with the melted butter. Bake for 14 to 16 minutes, or until browned on the top and bottom.

4. Remove from oven and sprinkle with the remaining ¼ cup cheese. Enjoy warm!

TOMATO-GINGER CHUTNEY

MAKES 3½ CUPS

¾ cup sugar

¾ cup apple cider vinegar

½ teaspoon salt

4 cups cored, peeled, seeded, and chopped ripe tomatoes

1 medium red onion, finely chopped

6 cloves garlic, finely chopped

3 tablespoons peeled and finely chopped fresh ginger

½ teaspoon chipotle powder or chili powder

¼ cup golden raisins

¼ cup sliced almonds, toasted

1. In a large nonreactive saucepan, bring the sugar, vinegar, and salt to a boil over high heat. Reduce the heat to medium. Cook for about 10 minutes, or until reduced by half.

2. Stir in the tomatoes, onion, garlic, ginger, and chipotle powder. Simmer, stirring frequently, for about 30 minutes or until thickened.

3. Stir in the raisins and almonds. Remove from the heat. Cool, cover, and refrigerate until ready to serve.

MICHAEL SCHLOW
SCHLOW BURGER WITH COUSIN SHARI'S COLESLAW

I chose to make my onion-topped, horseradish-slathered "fat boy" Schlow Burger for the Bash in 2008 because it's the best burger I know how to make. It's also fairly simple to do at home. I guess the crowd loved it because I won the People's Choice Award, the top honor of the evening. Grab a cold beer or iced tea with this one and get ready to make a mess—this is not a dainty meal!

SERVES 2

18 ounces 80% lean ground beef

2 tablespoons extra-virgin olive oil

Salt and freshly ground black pepper

¼ cup mayonnaise

Juice of ½ lemon

2 teaspoons prepared white horseradish

2 thick slices Vermont or English cheddar cheese

2 brioche hamburger buns, split and toasted

Crispy Onions (recipe follows)

Cousin Shari's Coleslaw (recipe follows)

1. Combine the meat and the oil in a mixing bowl. Season with salt and plenty of black pepper. Divide the meat into two 9-ounce portions and form them into patties. Place them on a plate, cover it with plastic wrap, and refrigerate until ready to use, up to 1 hour.

2. Heat a grill to high. In a mixing bowl, combine the mayonnaise, lemon juice, and horseradish; season with pepper. Cover with plastic wrap and refrigerate until ready to use.

3. Remove the patties from the refrigerator, and let them stand at room temperature for 5 to 7 minutes before grilling. Grill for 1½ minutes for rare meat. Give the patties a quarter turn to mark them, and cook for 1½ minutes more. Flip and cook for another 1½ minutes. Rotate a quarter turn and cook for 1½ minutes more. Transfer the hamburgers to the top shelf of a gas grill or to a cooler section on a charcoal grill, and cover each with a slice of cheese. If using a gas grill, turn off the heat. Cover the grill. Cook for 4 minutes more, or until the cheese has melted and the hamburgers are rare to medium-rare.

4. Spread plenty of the horseradish sauce on each hamburger; it should drip down the sides. Top each with some Crispy Onions. Season with pepper. Slather more sauce on the other half of the bun, and place it on top of the hamburger. Serve with Cousin Shari's Coleslaw.

recipe continues

CRISPY ONIONS

2 cups canola oil

1 large yellow onion, sliced into ⅛- to ⅓-inch-thick rings

1. Pour the oil into a small pot, add the onions, and bring to a boil over high heat. Reduce the heat to medium and cook at a very low simmer until the sugars in the onions are released and in essence melt. Turn the onions with a fork every 30 seconds. Cook for 12 to 15 minutes, or until golden brown. Adjust the heat as needed to maintain a low simmer.

2. Remove the onions from the oil and arrange them in a single layer on paper towels. At this point the onions won't be crispy, but I promise you that after a few minutes, as the caramelized sugars cool and harden, the onions will become deliciously crisp.

COUSIN SHARI'S COLESLAW

SERVES 4 TO 6

1 medium yellow onion, diced

1 cup sugar

1 cup pure or extra-virgin olive oil

⅔ cup mayonnaise

½ cup apple cider vinegar

1 teaspoon salt

½ teaspoon freshly ground black pepper

1 large head of green cabbage, shredded

1. Combine the onion and the sugar in a large mixing bowl, and let sit for 30 minutes.

2. Add the oil, mayonnaise, vinegar, salt, and pepper, and stir well to combine.

3. Add the cabbage 15 to 30 minutes before serving. Toss well and refrigerate until serving time.

GRILLED FOR ONE MINUTE
SPIKE MENDELSOHN

Q: Your first time at SoBe [2009], you won three out of four Burger Bash awards. What gives?

A: I couldn't believe it! Here I am, this twenty-eight-year-old guy up against all these amazing chefs! It just proved to me how far I've come, not only to be asked to compete but to win and win big. The best win, I have to say, is the People's Choice Award. It doesn't get any better than when customers leave happy and you're the one that fed 'em!

Q: We heard you had some prep issues. What happened?

A: The meat purveyor and I had an e-mail misunderstanding. I wanted my meat blend in 2.5-ounce patties—not frozen. They came in pressed by a machine, really really thin, not handcrafted at all. So my friends and I worked to defrost them with our bare hands all night long—2,000 frozen patties! Then we reblended them with more meat and re-pattied them the way I wanted.

Q: We hear that Mrs. Obama and the kids love to eat at your Washington restaurant. What's that like? Any advance warning?

A: No advance warning more than a few minutes. They show up and we love it—that's why my staff is always on its game. You know someone special is coming when the Secret Service advance team appears. Okay, I guess that's the warning!

Q: Do they pay?

A: Of course! No free rides here!

Q: Why the name "Spike"?

A: Because my real name, Evangelos, would get me beat up! There was a kid in school who wore bandanas and one day lost a tooth; I called him Rambo. So he got back at me because my hair was spiked.

Q: Any personal or professional fantasy or goal not yet attained?

A: My own TV show—are you network people hearing me? Make a dream come true! And a boat and a beach house.

Q: Who would you most love to go up against on *Iron Chef* . . . and why?

A: Well, let's see . . . I took down Flay and Morimoto already when I won the Burger Bash! That leaves Cat Cora and Michael Symon. I'd have to say Symon because I used to work in his restaurant, as a butcher, and we both have that Greek blood in our veins. Plus we both have a great sense of humor and a laid-back approach to cooking.

SPIKE MENDELSOHN
COLLETTI'S SMOKEHOUSE BURGER AND TOASTED MARSHMALLOW SHAKE

My first year at the Burger Bash was 2009 and we won three of the four awards—it was insane! My team and I put so much hard work into the event and I'm so happy it paid off. So here's our winning burger, which we served slider-size. In our restaurant, Good Stuff Eatery, it's on the permanent menu and it's one of my three best sellers. It's named for chef Mike Colletti, a family friend who works with us, and personally, it's my favorite. There's something about the combination—the sauce, sharp cheddar, bacon, crisp Vidalias—that just sings. Delicious! And since I love a great shake almost as much as a burger, I skipped the fries and served this shake as my go-with instead. It's like a campfire in your mouth!

SERVES 6

2 pounds ground sirloin

Canola oil

1 pound sliced applewood-smoked bacon

Salt and freshly ground black pepper

6 slices cheddar cheese

6 potato buns, split and toasted

1½ cups Chipotle Barbecue Sauce (recipe follows)

Cliff's Homegrown Vidalia Onion Petals (recipe follows)

Toasted Marshmallow Shakes (recipe follows), for serving

1. Divide the meat into six 5-ounce balls and form them into patties. Place the patties on a baking sheet, cover with plastic wrap, and refrigerate until ready to use.

2. Heat a large skillet over medium-high heat. Add enough oil to just cover the entire bottom of the skillet. When the oil begins to smoke, add the bacon. Cook until crispy. Remove, using a slotted spoon, and place on paper towels to drain.

3. Reduce the heat under the skillet to medium, and place the patties in the skillet. Season with salt and pepper, and cook for 3 minutes. Turn, and season the other side of the hamburgers. Cook for 3 minutes. During the last 2 minutes of cooking, divide the bacon over the patties and top them with a slice of cheese. Cover the pan with a lid during the last 30 seconds, and cook the hamburgers until the cheese has melted.

4. Remove the hamburgers from the heat and place a patty on the bottom half of each toasted bun. Top each patty with some barbecue sauce, Onion Petals, and the top half of a bun. Wrap the sandwiches in wax paper and serve, with the shakes alongside.

recipe continues

136

CHIPOTLE BARBECUE SAUCE

MAKES 3 CUPS

1 7-ounce can chipotle chiles in adobo sauce

2 cups sweet, mild barbecue sauce

½ cup ketchup

4 tablespoons apple cider vinegar

1 tablespoon molasses

In a blender, blend half of the chiles and adobo sauce until smooth. Add the barbecue sauce, ketchup, vinegar, and molasses. Puree until smooth. Strain through a fine-mesh strainer into a bowl. Refrigerate until ready to use.

CLIFF'S HOMEGROWN VIDALIA ONION PETALS

SERVES 4

ONION RING BATTER

2 cups all-purpose flour

1 tablespoon salt

1 tablespoon bittersweet paprika

1 tablespoon dark (packed) brown sugar

½ tablespoon Old Bay seasoning

½ teaspoon ground cumin

Pinch of freshly ground black pepper

Pinch of cayenne pepper

1 cup beer

1 cup buttermilk

1 large egg, lightly beaten

Canola oil, for frying

4 Vidalia onions, each sliced into 8 wedges

1 cup all-purpose flour

Salt and freshly ground black pepper

FOR THE BATTER

1. In a large bowl, sift together the flour, salt, paprika, brown sugar, Old Bay seasoning, cumin, black pepper, and cayenne. Set aside.

2. In another bowl, whisk the beer, buttermilk, and egg together. Gradually add the dry ingredients, whisking until there are no lumps. Cover with plastic wrap and refrigerate until ready to use, or up to one day in advance.

TO COOK THE ONIONS

1. Line a baking sheet with paper towels. Set it aside.

2. Heat about 3 inches of oil in a large, deep skillet until it reads 350°F on an instant-read thermometer.

3. Meanwhile, remove the batter from the refrigerator and uncover it. Place the onions in a large bowl, add the flour, and toss to coat. Shake off any excess flour. Dip the onions in the batter, coating them well. Add the onions to the skillet one by one, making sure not to overcrowd the skillet. Cook until golden brown and crispy, about 3 minutes per side. Using a slotted spoon, remove the petals and place them on the reserved baking sheet to drain.

4. Season with salt and pepper, and serve immediately on Colletti's Smokehouse Burgers.

TOASTED MARSHMALLOW SHAKE

SERVES 4

1 1-pound bag jumbo marshmallows

2 cups whole milk

2 cups creamy vanilla ice cream

1 tablespoon sour cream

1. Heat the broiler in the oven.

2. Reserve 4 of the marshmallows to use as a garnish. Spread the remaining marshmallows on a cookie sheet. Place the cookie sheet under the broiler and toast the marshmallows until charred. Remove from the oven and set aside to cool.

3. Place the remaining 4 marshmallows on another baking sheet and broil, turning them once, for about 1 minute, or until toasted and slightly golden. Remove from the oven and set aside to cool.

4. Combine the milk, ice cream, sour cream, and charred marshmallows in a blender, and blend for 5 minutes. Divide among four 8-ounce glasses. Garnish each glass with a reserved toasted marshmallow.

"SPIKE DEFINITELY IMPRESSED ME AS SOMEBODY WHO WAS OUT TO WIN. HE TOOK IT VERY SERIOUSLY AND WANTED TO MAKE A VERY HIGH-QUALITY BURGER. HE AND I SPOKE MANY MANY TIMES BEFORE THE BURGER BASH AND DISCUSSED ALL THE SMALLEST DETAILS. A TOTAL PROFESSIONAL."

—RANDY FISHER, BURGER BASH EVENT MANAGER

KATIE LEE
LOGAN COUNTY HAMBURGERS kid friendly

Everyone was kind of shocked when I beat out all the big-name chefs and won the New York Wine & Food Fest Burger Bash with this simple patty melt in 2008. The critics said it's a sandwich, not a burger. But I say: ground beef, melted cheese, grilled bread, and butter—what's not a burger about that? Anyway, I made it again for the SoBe Burger Bash the following year . . . and won nothing! Still, I had tons of fun. This thin little burger is named for my grandmother, who was raised in Depression-era Logan County, West Virginia. Money was scarce and meat had to go a long way.

SERVES 6

1 pound 85% lean ground beef

1 medium yellow onion: half grated and the other half thinly sliced

1 large egg, lightly beaten

1 teaspoon kosher salt

1 teaspoon freshly ground black pepper

¼ teaspoon garlic powder

2 tablespoons unsalted butter, at room temperature

12 slices white bread

12 slices American cheese (optional)

Ketchup, for serving

Mustard, for serving

Sandwich pickles, for serving

1. In a medium bowl, combine the meat, grated onion, egg, salt, pepper, and garlic powder. Form into 6 thin patties.

2. Heat a large, heavy-bottomed skillet over medium-high heat. Cook the patties for about 3 minutes per side, or until browned. Remove from the pan and place on paper towels to drain. Set aside. Drain the grease from the skillet.

3. Spread the butter on one side of each slice of bread. Place 6 slices, butter side down, in the skillet. Top each with a slice of cheese, if desired, sliced onions, and a burger patty. Top with the remaining cheese, if desired, and a final slice of bread, butter side up.

4. Cook for about 2 minutes per side, or until golden brown. Remove from the heat and serve with mustard, ketchup, pickles, or any other desired hamburger toppings.

"SUN, SAND, FOOD, AND FUN—THAT'S WHY WE ALL WANT TO COME TO SOBE! IT'S MY FAVORITE WEEKEND OF THE WINTER."

—KATIE LEE

MICHAEL SYMON
FAT DOUG BURGER

I owe it all to pastrami! I created this burger in honor of my partner, Doug Petkovic—he's a huge fan of pastrami and is always in search of the best sandwich—and it won the People's Choice Award at the Burger Bash in 2010. Although Doug is rather svelte, this burger is fat, juicy, and delicious.

SERVES 4

SLAW

½ head Napa cabbage, shredded

½ clove garlic, minced

½ small red onion, thinly sliced

½ fresh jalapeño pepper, minced

3 tablespoons champagne vinegar

1 tablespoon Dijon mustard

2 tablespoons mayonnaise

1 tablespoon sugar

1½ teaspoons salt

1 tablespoon Worcestershire sauce

1 tablespoon ShaSha Sauce (recipe follows)

BURGERS

½ pound ground sirloin

½ pound ground brisket

½ pound ground boneless short rib or 1½ pounds ground beef (75% lean and 25% fat or 80% lean and 20% fat)

Salt and freshly ground black pepper

½ pound pastrami, thinly sliced

4 slices Swiss cheese, medium thick

1½ tablespoons butter, melted

4 brioche or egg buns, split

FOR THE SLAW

In a medium bowl, mix together the cabbage, garlic, onion, jalapeño, vinegar, mustard, mayonnaise, sugar, salt, Worcestershire sauce, and ShaSha Sauce. Cover, and refrigerate for 1 hour.

FOR THE BURGERS

1. Build a charcoal fire or heat a gas grill.

2. On a work surface, combine the meats and form the burgers into 4 equal-size patties. Season liberally with salt and pepper.

3. Grill the burgers over high heat, 3 to 5 minutes per side, or until medium-rare.

4. Meanwhile, heat a large sauté pan over medium heat. Place 4 heaping piles of pastrami in the pan. After 2 minutes, top each pile with a slice of Swiss cheese. Remove them when the cheese is melted; set aside.

5. Pour the butter into the pan. Place the buns in the pan, cut side down, and toast, about 2 minutes.

6. Place a heaping tablespoon of the slaw on the bottom half of each bun. Top with a burger and a mound of pastrami and cheese. Cover each with the top half of the bun, and serve immediately.

SHASHA SAUCE

MAKES 3 CUPS

12 hot banana peppers from a jar, tops removed, chopped

4 garlic cloves

1 cup yellow mustard

1 cup white wine vinegar

½ cup sugar

2 tablespoons all-purpose flour

½ cup water

1. In a food processor, puree the peppers, garlic cloves, mustard, and vinegar.

2. Pour the puree into a nonreactive saucepan, then add the sugar and bring it to a boil over high heat. Lower the heat and simmer the mixture for 30 minutes.

3. In a small bowl or juice glass, mix the flour and water to a smooth paste. Whisk it into the pepper mixture and continue to simmer for 20 minutes, stirring regularly, until it becomes very thick. Let the sauce cool, then pour it into a covered, nonreactive container (such as a glass jar). The sauce can be refrigerated for up to 1 month.

"THERE IS NO GREATER SPECTACLE IN THE HAMBURGER UNIVERSE THAN THE ANNUAL RACHAEL RAY BURGER BASH . . ."

—JOSH OZERSKY, *TIME* MAGAZINE, MARCH 2010

CHAPTER 5
COMFORT AND CASUAL FOOD

OPPOSITE: (From left to right) Claire Robinson and Katie Lee,
2010. Martha Stewart received SoBe's Lifetime Achievement Award
in 2007.

When I was young and just starting out in the business, my dream was to be able to afford a meal at French Laundry—and to be able to get a reservation.

Now that I can, I'd oftentimes rather have a burger at Taylor's Automatic Refresher on Highway 29 in nearby St. Helena. (But I still think Thomas Keller is an awesome chef!)

People assume, because of my work, that my life is one endless three-star meal and one elegant party after another. And they're right, somewhat. I dine in very nice restaurants—*very* nice—very often. Sometimes five or six nights a week. But like many people in the food business, that's not my favorite way to eat.

For me, the simpler the food, the better.

People often say that they're afraid to invite me over for dinner, but I say if you can make a great meat loaf, a great burger, a great London broil, you can make me happy. If I had my choice, my last meal on earth would be chef Art Smith's fried chicken and a chocolate chip cookie from Levain Bakery in New York.

And most of my chef friends feel the same way, particularly when they gather to eat late at night. Chances are you'll find them devouring steaming bowls of pho or sushi or oysters or burgers or pasta or roast chicken or omelets—anything but "fancy" food. (Daniel Boulud's late-night scrambled-egg parties are legendary.)

While the SoBe festival offers more than its share of chic evenings and elegant meals, we're still, at our heart, one big beach party—and that calls for casual, festive, stressless food. And we make sure to offer it in every delicious permutation possible, morning, noon, and night. Our guests love that about us, and so do our chefs.

"There's no need to make any restaurant reservations during the festival," says Katie Lee. "I like wandering around the Grand Tasting tent and sampling all of the chefs' food and sneaking backstage at the demos to eat leftovers. The vibe is so laid-back and casual, perfect for a day of nibbling instead of a big production of a meal."

"SoBe, more than any of the hundreds of events I've participated in, so beautifully illustrates how wonderful it is when people

come together through food," says chef Don Pintabona. "I think the absence of formality and the addition of sun and sand work wonders in letting folks appreciate their friends around a shared table."

Sifting through the hundreds of recipes submitted for this book, it quickly became clear that we'd need a chapter for recipes like these. Call it comfort or casual or soul food: we all know it when we eat it. Food without attitude. Shoes-off, feet-up fare. And when top chefs take on casual food, the results can be spectacular. Here are some laid-back dishes I know you'll love as much as I do.

PADMA LAKSHMI
SAUTÉED SWEET POTATO AND EDAMAME

This is a lovely, colorful dish that pairs well with roasts and heartier main dishes. It's very easy to prepare and is quite popular with kids and grown-ups alike. It's also an unexpected twist on a holiday classic. Pair it with your next Thanksgiving turkey for a spicier version of the classic sweet potato side dish.

SERVES 6 TO 8

1½ pounds sweet potatoes

1 pound frozen shelled edamame

1½ teaspoons vegetable oil

1 teaspoon black mustard seeds

1 teaspoon cumin seeds

1 whole dried red chile

1 onion, chopped

2 cloves garlic, sliced

1 tablespoon minced peeled fresh ginger

Salt

2 tablespoons freshly squeezed lemon or lime juice

½ cup chopped fresh cilantro

1. Boil the sweet potatoes in enough water to just cover them for about 25 minutes, or until tender. At the same time, in another saucepan, boil the edamame in just enough water to cover for 15 to 20 minutes.

2. Drain the edamame. Drain the potatoes, and once they are cool enough to touch, peel and dice them.

3. Heat the oil in a frying pan over medium heat. Add the mustard seeds. When they pop and start to crackle out of the pan, add the cumin seeds, chile, onion, garlic, and ginger. Stir well. Let the onion turn golden brown; then add the reserved edamame and stir. Add the sweet potatoes. Mix all the ingredients well and sauté for just a few minutes more to mingle the tastes evenly. Season with salt to taste. Add the lemon juice and stir. Garnish by sprinkling the cilantro over the top. Serve warm.

GRILLED FOR ONE MINUTE
PADMA LAKSHMI

Q: What are three cookbooks you couldn't live without?

A: *The Talisman of Happiness* by Ada Boni, which really isn't a cookbook; *How to Cook a Wolf* by M. F. K. Fisher, and *The Art of Eating,* which contains that and other writing by M. F. K. Fisher; and anything by Edna Lewis, the late great Southern cookbook author.

Q: What do you eat when no one is watching?

A: I don't care who watches anytime I eat anything (which is obvious by now, I guess).

Q: If you were to open a restaurant, what would it look like and what would you serve?

A: I always wanted to do a cozy late-night diner for South Asian/Indian street food. Something part Indochine, part Mr. Chow, but very low-key, like Raoul's. I'd serve tapas from around the world as well as comfort spicy stewy food and all types of street food.

" THE FESTIVAL IS AN UNBELIEVABLE WINNER. IT HELPS THE STUDENTS, THE UNIVERSITY, THE COMMUNITY, THE CITY, OUR BRANDS, AND OUR SUPPLIERS. IT'S BEEN SUCCESSFUL ABOVE AND BEYOND OUR WILDEST EXPECTATIONS. "

—WAYNE CHAPLIN, CEO, SOUTHERN WINE & SPIRITS

"I LOOK FORWARD TO SOUTH BEACH EVERY YEAR. I'M ALWAYS IMPRESSED BY THE GENEROSITY OF THE HOST CHEFS, WHO OPEN THEIR KITCHENS TO VISITING CREWS SO THEY TOO CAN SERVE THEIR BEST. NOW THAT I HAVE MY OWN RESTAURANT IN MIAMI BEACH, I'M THRILLED TO GIVE BACK AND CONTINUE THIS TRADITION."

—LAURENT TOURONDEL

LAURENT TOURONDEL
BLT GRILLED TUNA SANDWICH

This is my hands-down favorite BLT. It combines the flavors of a classic (juicy tomato, crisp bacon, peppery arugula, creamy mayonnaise) with the flavors of a perfect tuna Niçoise (seared tuna, tapenade, red onion, hard-cooked egg) to create a flavorful and colorful sandwich. It's been on the menu at the BLT Fish Shack in New York since we opened, and it's still my favorite item to order whenever I'm there.

SERVES 6

1½ pounds yellowfin tuna, cut into 12 slices about ⅓-inch thick

Fine sea salt and freshly ground black pepper

½ cup olive oil

4 teaspoons freshly squeezed lemon juice

½ teaspoon chopped garlic

1 large bunch arugula, tough stems removed (about 2 cups)

½ cup mayonnaise

¼ cup black olive tapenade

1 loaf rustic Italian bread, cut into twelve ½-inch-thick diagonal slices, toasted

12 slices applewood-smoked bacon, cooked until crisp

1 medium red onion, sliced

2 ripe tomatoes, sliced

3 hard-boiled eggs, peeled and sliced

6 ounces Parmigiano-Reggiano cheese, cut into thin slices with a vegetable peeler or a mandoline

1 ripe avocado, preferably Hass, pitted, peeled, and sliced

1 bunch fresh basil, tough stems removed

1. Heat a grill pan or outdoor grill to high. Sprinkle the tuna on both sides with salt and pepper. Place the tuna on the pan or grill rack and cook for 1 to 2 minutes per side, or until rare to medium-rare, depending on your preference. Set the tuna aside.

2. In a medium bowl, whisk together the oil, lemon juice, garlic, and salt and pepper to taste. Add the arugula and toss well.

3. To assemble the sandwiches, spread some mayonnaise and tapenade on each slice of bread. Divide the bacon, onion, tomatoes, eggs, cheese, and avocado among half of the slices. Top with the tuna, the basil, and the arugula salad. Cover with the remaining bread.

4. Cut the sandwiches in half and serve immediately.

Chef's Tip: To make these sandwiches easier to eat, wrap them in butcher paper or waxed paper. For a change, substitute pesto for the tapenade.

TED ALLEN
BAKED SHRIMP "SCAMPI" ON ZUCCHINI CARPACCIO

Here's a delicious twist on the classic scampi, with a beautiful and easy presentation. For the best impact, select a white or other solid-color square or rectangular salad plate. Then, trim the ends of the zucchini so it fits perfectly within the plate's borders. Slice the squash paper-thin with a mandoline or a vegetable peeler; then arrange the slices, overlapping slightly, to fill the plate. Or, if you prefer, arrange the slices in a basket-weave pattern. Either way, it's a great look!

SERVES 4 AS AN APPETIZER OR A LIGHT LUNCH

2 medium zucchini

5 tablespoons extra-virgin olive oil

2 tablespoons freshly squeezed lemon juice

2 teaspoons grated lemon zest

1½ teaspoons sea salt

¼ teaspoon sugar

½ teaspoon plus 2 pinches of freshly ground black pepper

16 to 20 medium shrimp, peeled and deveined, tails on

1 tablespoon dry white wine

6 tablespoons unsalted butter, at room temperature

2 cloves garlic, minced

1 tablespoon minced fresh flat-leaf parsley

1 tablespoon minced fresh basil, tarragon, or thyme

Pinch of red pepper flakes

1 large egg yolk

⅓ cup panko bread crumbs

1. Trim the ends from the zucchini. Using a mandoline or a vegetable peeler, cut the zucchini into paper-thin slices. Arrange 6 to 9 slices on each plate, in rows or in a basket-weave pattern. Reserve the leftover zucchini pieces for another use.

2. In a mixing bowl, whisk together 3 tablespoons of the oil, 1 tablespoon of the lemon juice, 1 teaspoon of the zest, ¼ teaspoon of the salt, the sugar, and a pinch of pepper. Drizzle the vinaigrette over the zucchini and allow to rest for at least 15 minutes to soften and flavor the zucchini.

3. Heat the oven to 425°F.

4. In a mixing bowl, combine the shrimp with the remaining 2 tablespoons oil, the wine, 1 teaspoon of the salt, and the ½ teaspoon pepper; toss, and set aside to marinate for 15 minutes.

5. In a small bowl, mash together the butter, garlic, herbs, red pepper flakes, remaining 1 teaspoon zest, remaining 1 tablespoon lemon juice, the egg yolk, panko, remaining ¼ teaspoon salt, and remaining pinch of pepper. Set aside.

6. Remove the shrimp from the wine marinade. Nestle 4 to 5 shrimp together as if "spooning" and thread onto a bamboo skewer. Repeat with the remaining shrimp. Trim the skewers with scissors to fit on the serving plates.

7. Place the shrimp in a baking dish. Drizzle with the remaining marinade, and top with the butter mixture. Bake for 10 to 12 minutes.

8. Place 1 shrimp skewer atop each zucchini carpaccio, and serve.

MARTHA STEWART
LOBSTER ROLL

A big pot of boiling lobsters always draws a crowd, and when I demoed this at SoBe, that was no exception. When you're making a lobster roll, the fewer the ingredients, the better and more authentic your sandwich will be. Some people prefer to add just mayonnaise or melted butter, but a sprinkling of fresh herbs can be delicious—just nothing too strong like rosemary or thyme. Fresh lemon juice is also a great addition. Not only is lobster meat utterly delicious, it's low-calorie and very nutritious. Butter the buns on the outside (the Maine way), toast them in a skillet, and load them up. The more meat you put in, the more popular you'll be.

MAKES 8 ROLLS

1½ pounds cooked shelled lobster meat (from about four 1½-pound lobsters), chopped into ½-inch pieces

2 tablespoons homemade or good-quality store-bought mayonnaise

½ teaspoon finely chopped fresh chives (optional)

½ teaspoon finely chopped fresh tarragon or chervil (optional)

1 teaspoon freshly squeezed lemon juice, or to taste

Coarse salt (use sea salt if you have some) and freshly ground black pepper

8 top-split hot-dog buns

2 tablespoons butter, melted

1. Stir the lobster, mayonnaise, and herbs (if using) together in a large bowl. Add the lemon juice, and season with salt and pepper to taste. Cover and refrigerate the salad for up to 2 hours.

2. Lightly brush the outsides of the buns with the butter, and cook on a hot griddle or in a heavy skillet until golden brown, about 1½ minutes per side.

3. Spoon about ½ cup of the lobster mixture into each bun, and serve immediately.

❝ I LOVE TO COME TO SOBE, AND I SEE IT AS AN HONOR TO BE ASKED. IT GIVES US A GREAT CHANCE TO TALK TO OUR FANS—AND WHAT A BEAUTIFUL VENUE. ❞

—MARTHA STEWART

GRILLED FOR ONE MINUTE
MICHAEL CHIARELLO

Q: What was the moment when you knew you wanted to be a chef?

A: With my mom standing over me holding my hand and thumb, teaching me to make gnocchi!

Q: Have you ever been fired? From where and why?

A: Almost. As a young buck working at the Grand Bay Hotel in Coconut Grove, Florida, I admonished the managing director for walking past a room service tray in the hall . . . ouch! It was one of our service mantras: everyone pours coffee, opens doors, picks up trays in the hallway. But chastising your boss's boss is not the way to work your way up the ladder! I was hired by the corporate office, so my scolding came from the president and VP of the company—quite a lesson in humility!

Q: What is your best advice for an aspiring chef?

A: Work for the best chef you can, for whatever he'll pay you, and add one hour of work for free for every hour you get paid.

Q: What is the worst kitchen disaster you remember or the worst day of your culinary career?

A: My first big party, I was asked to cook for a very high-profile benefit in a million-dollar home. The pig I was roasting leaked onto the bottom of the oven and then the oven caught fire, right in front of the guests. We saved the evening (barely) by covering the pig in a wet blanket and wrestling it into the garage, where we peeled off the burnt skin and then served it, but only after a blast of the fire extinguisher in the oven. It was a long evening of cleaning walls throughout the entire kitchen.

Q: Tell us about one personal or professional fantasy still unfulfilled.

A: To live four months a year in Italy, cooking, writing, and building a year's worth of ideas for my restaurant, Bottega, in Yountville. To have a place my children could come and go from, a place where they could not only learn Italian but also learn how to "be" Italian. It's a gift I was given (in California, but with my Italian family) that I would love to pass on.

Q: What do you love about SoBe?

A: I get the chance to cook a great demo, sign some books, pour our wines at Best of the Best (a huge honor), and hang with all my chef/wine buds.

HOWIE KLEINBERG
SHRIMP AND GRITS

When I was growing up and spending summers in North Carolina, I was heavily influenced by Southern and High Country cuisine, so this is my contemporary approach to a traditional BBQ favorite. This is now a mainstay on the menu at my restaurant, Bulldog Barbecue, in North Miami, and I served it (to wide acclaim!) at the BubbleQ in 2009. With it, a crisp, fruity, light chardonnay would be ideal.

SERVES 2 TO 4

1 pound shrimp, peeled and deveined

2 tablespoons Bulldog's dry rub (or other store-bought dry rub)

6 tablespoons extra-virgin olive oil

¼ cup chopped garlic

¼ cup chopped shallots

1 cup chicken stock

1 cup cooked hominy grits

¼ cup dry white wine

½ cup diced tomato

4 tablespoons butter

Salt and freshly ground black pepper

¾ to 1 cup heavy cream

6 tablespoons white cheddar cheese

2 tablespoons chopped fresh parsley

½ cup sliced scallions, white and tender green parts, for garnish

1. In a bowl, combine the shrimp with the dry rub and 3 tablespoons of the oil. Marinate in the refrigerator for 4 hours.

2. Heat a saucepan over medium heat. Add the remaining 3 tablespoons oil, half (2 tablespoons) of the garlic, and half (2 tablespoons) of the shallots; cook, stirring frequently, until translucent, 3 to 5 minutes. Add the stock and bring to a boil. Add the grits and cook, stirring constantly, until the stock has evaporated, about 10 minutes. Set aside.

3. Heat a sauté pan over high heat. Add the shrimp and sauté until opaque, 1½ to 2 minutes. Add the remaining 2 tablespoons garlic and the remaining 2 tablespoons shallots, and cook until translucent, about 1 minute. Deglaze the pan with the wine. Then add the tomato, swirl in 2 tablespoons of the butter, and season with salt and pepper. Set aside.

4. Return the grits to medium heat. Add the cream in ¼-cup increments, stirring constantly, until the texture is smooth and creamy. Add the cheese, remaining 2 tablespoons butter, and parsley, and heat through. Season with salt and pepper. Spoon the grits into 2 to 4 serving bowls and place the shrimp on top. Garnish with the scallions, and serve.

NORMAN VAN AKEN
CHILEAN SEAFOOD PASTEL

When Emeril asked me to be one of the guest chefs for his Tribute Dinner in 2009, I knew he wanted me to express my love of New World flavors. This seafood pastel (a kind of savory pie), my contribution to the menu, hails from South America. I discovered and adapted it while writing my cookbook *New World Kitchen*. In Chile, this dish would be called *pastel de mariscos,* which sounds more melodic and enticing.

SERVES 6 TO 8

1 tablespoon unsalted butter, melted

2 cups ½-inch dice of peeled calabaza or acorn squash

1 tablespoon sugar

1 teaspoon toasted and ground cumin seeds

Kosher salt and freshly ground black pepper

2 cups corn kernels (3 to 4 ears)

1 poblano chile, roasted, peeled, stemmed, seeded, and minced

10 ounces cooked smoked or cured chorizo or other favorite sausage, cut into small dice or crumbled

12 ounces shrimp, peeled and deveined

12 ounces snapper fillets, cut into 1-inch pieces

12 ounces sea bass fillets, cut into 1-inch pieces

2 tablespoons pure olive oil

1 tablespoon unsalted butter

SAUCE

1 tablespoon unsalted butter

4 cloves garlic, sliced

4 shallots, minced

¼ cup chopped fresh flat-leaf parsley

1½ cups dry white wine

1 cup sour cream

Salt and freshly ground black pepper

CORN CRUST BATTER

2 tablespoons unsalted butter

2 cloves garlic, sliced

2½ cups corn kernels (3 to 4 ears)

1 extra-large egg

1 extra-large egg yolk

¼ cup milk

¼ cup all-purpose flour

½ teaspoon baking powder

1 teaspoon kosher salt, plus more to taste

1½ tablespoons unsalted butter

6 scallions (white and green parts), minced

1 jalapeño, stemmed, seeded, and minced

Salt and freshly ground black pepper

½ cup dry bread crumbs

1. Heat the oven to 375°F.

2. In a medium bowl, toss together the melted butter, squash, sugar, and cumin. Season with salt and pepper; place in a shallow baking dish. Roast for 25 to 35 minutes, until the squash is tender.

3. Remove the dish from the oven and stir in the corn. Return to the oven and toast for 10 minutes.

4. Remove the baking dish from the oven and stir in the poblano and chorizo; reserve. Turn the oven temperature down to 350°F.

5. Season the shrimp and fish with salt and pepper. Heat the oil and butter in a large nonstick sauté pan over medium-high heat. Once the butter foams, add the shrimp and cook until opaque, 3 minutes. Transfer the shrimp to a plate. Add the fish to the pan and sauté, gently shaking the pan so it doesn't stick, until browned all over, 2 minutes. Using a slotted spoon, transfer the fish to a separate plate.

FOR THE SAUCE

Melt the butter in a saucepan over medium-high heat. Add the garlic and shallots and sauté for 1 minute. Stir in the parsley and wine, and reduce the liquid to approximately ½ cup. (As the seafood rests, some juices may accumulate in the plates; pour them into the reducing wine.) Whisk in the sour cream. Season with salt and pepper, and remove from the heat.

TO FINISH THE FILLING

Cut the shrimp into bite-size pieces, and toss it with the squash mixture and the fish. Gently fold in the sauce, and set aside while you make the batter for the crust.

FOR THE CORN CRUST BATTER

1. Melt the butter in a nonstick sauté pan over medium-high heat. Sauté the garlic for 1 minute, then add the corn and cook for 3 to 4 minutes. Remove from the heat and let cool.

2. Combine the corn with the egg, egg yolk, and milk in a blender, and process until smooth.

3. Sift the flour, baking powder, and salt together into a medium bowl. Pour in the egg mixture, folding the flour mixture into it with a spatula. Set the batter aside.

TO MAKE THE PASTEL

1. In a small sauté pan, melt the butter over medium heat. Sauté the scallions and jalapeño for 2 minutes, or until the scallions are bright green and starting to soften. Season with salt and pepper, and reserve.

2. Dust the bottom of a 12-inch ovenproof sauté pan with the bread crumbs. Spread the filling evenly over the bread crumbs. Spread the corn crust batter over the filling, and sprinkle the sautéed scallions and jalapeños over the top. Bake for 50 minutes, or until the center of the pie springs back to the touch.

3. Serve hot, cut into wedges.

JAMIE OLIVER
ROASTED CARROTS AND BEETS WITH THE JUICIEST PORK CHOPS kid friendly

More often than not, when you mention carrots and beets the first image that pops into a person's head will be of horrible-tasting vegetables boiled to within an inch of their lives. But when carrots and beets are roasted, their natural sugars cook out and the result is beautiful, tasty vegetables that go wonderfully with big juicy pork chops. Chuck a few smashed garlic cloves, a woody herb like rosemary, thyme, sage, or bay, and a splash of vinegar or lemon juice into the roasting tray and you'll never look back.

SERVES 4

1½ pounds carrots, mixed colors if available, peeled

1½ pounds beets, different sizes and colors if available

Sea salt

1 whole bulb of garlic, broken apart: half the cloves smashed, half left whole

Extra-virgin olive oil

Freshly ground black pepper

Juice of 1 orange

A few sprigs fresh thyme, leaves picked off and reserved

A few sprigs fresh rosemary, leaves picked off and reserved

5 tablespoons balsamic vinegar

4 thick organic pork loin chops, skin on

8 fresh sage leaves

1 lemon

1. Heat the oven to 425°F.

2. Put your carrots into a large pot and your beets into another, and add enough water to both pots to cover the vegetables. Season with salt and bring to a boil. Cook for 15 to 20 minutes, or until just tender; then drain and place in separate bowls. Peel your beets, and cut any larger carrots and beets in half or into quarters. Smaller ones can stay whole.

3. Now add your flavorings while the vegetables are still hot: Toss the carrots with half the smashed garlic and a glug of oil, then lightly season with salt and pepper. Add the orange juice and the thyme leaves, and toss again. Mix the beets with the rest of the smashed garlic, the rosemary, and the vinegar, and season with salt and pepper. You can now put the veg either into separate ovenproof dishes, or together in a large roasting pan with the carrots in one half of the pan and the beets in the other. Place in the middle of the oven and roast for about 30 minutes, or until starting to turn golden.

4. While the carrots and beets are cooking, lay the chops on a board and score through the skin and the streaky-looking part of the meat. This will give you lovely crackling. Firmly press a sage leaf onto the eye meat on both sides of each chop. Season with salt and pepper.

5. When the vegetables are starting to color, heat a large ovenproof frying pan or small roasting pan on a burner, add a good glug of oil, and put in the chops. As soon as you've got nice color on one side, turn the chops over and place the pan in the oven. Roast for 10 minutes, or until the chops are crisp on the outside and just cooked through and juicy in the middle. Remove the chops to a warmed plate.

6. Pour most of the fat away from the pan and add a squeeze of lemon juice to it. Stir and scrape the lovely sticky bits off the bottom, and drizzle this sauce all over the chops.

7. Remove the carrots and beets from the oven (they should be nice and sticky by now). Serve them with the chops and a glass of wine.

"SOBE? THE WHOLE EVENT WAS AN INCREDIBLE BUZZ. I LEARNED SO MUCH FROM TALKING TO GREAT CHEFS FROM ALL OVER THE WORLD."

—JAMIE OLIVER

DON PINTABONA
CAVATELLI PASTA WITH PEAS, PROSCIUTTO, AND RICOTTA CHEESE

When I was celebrating birthdays as a child, my mom would let me choose what I'd like for my special dinner. My choice was always cavatelli, in varying preparations, and this version was always my favorite. My grandmother would make the dough, I'd make the little pasta "bullets" on her well-worn hand-crank machine, and Mom would finish the preparation.

SERVES 4 TO 6

Salt

1 pound homemade cavatelli (recipe follows) or dried store-bought

1 Spanish onion, cut into small dice

3 tablespoons olive oil

3 cloves garlic, thinly sliced

2 cups pear tomatoes (red and yellow), halved

2 ounces prosciutto, julienned

1 tablespoon freshly ground black pepper

8 ounces fresh garden peas, shelled and blanched

2 tablespoons unsalted butter, at room temperature

1 teaspoon red pepper flakes (optional)

½ cup (about 4 ounces) ricotta cheese

2 tablespoons julienned fresh mint leaves

Freshly grated Parmigiano-Reggiano cheese, for serving (optional)

1. Bring a large pot of salted water to a boil. Add the pasta and stir to prevent it from sticking together. Boil the pasta for about 3 minutes, or until it floats to the top.

2. Meanwhile, in a large sauté pan set over moderate heat, sauté the onion in the oil for about 1 minute, or until it is translucent. Add the garlic and sauté until golden. Then quickly add the tomatoes and prosciutto to stop the cooking process.

3. Season with salt and pepper, and toss gently until the tomatoes wilt and release their juices. Add the peas and toss to mix. Set aside.

4. When the pasta is ready, drain it, reserving ½ cup of the pasta water. Toss the pasta in a bowl with the butter, and season with salt and pepper.

5. Add the tomato mixture to the pasta, and add the reserved pasta water as needed to moisten it. Toss well. Taste, and adjust the seasoning. Add the red pepper flakes, if desired.

6. Divide the pasta among warm pasta bowls. Place a nice dollop of ricotta on top of each dish, and garnish with the mint. Sprinkle with some Parmigiano-Reggiano, if desired.

recipe continues

CAVATELLI

MAKES 1 POUND

1½ cups all-purpose flour

½ cup semolina flour

½ teaspoon salt

1 large egg, beaten

8 ounces ricotta cheese

1. Sift together the flour, semolina, and salt.

2. Add all the ingredients to a bowl of a mixer fitted with a dough hook attachment.

3. Knead the dough in the mixer on medium speed until it forms a ball.

4. Remove the dough from the bowl, wrap the ball in plastic wrap, and refrigerate for 30 minutes.

5. Form the cavatelli on a cavatelli machine, following the manufacturer's directions.

Note: Fresh cavatelli are perishable because of the ricotta and eggs in the dough, but will last 3 to 4 days in the fridge. Cavatelli freeze well: wrap them tightly in zip-lock bags and freeze for up to 3 months.

"WHEN LEE LAUNCHED THE SOBE FESTIVAL, HE SEEMED TO ME A DOGGED VISIONARY, A PASSIONATE MAGICIAN. HE GATHERS AMAZING TALENT TO THE BEACH, AND EACH YEAR I REALLY LOOK FORWARD TO IT. NOT JUST TO SEE OLD FRIENDS, BUT TO BE PART OF LEE'S WHOLE BEWITCHING WORLD."
—DANA COWIN, EDITOR IN CHIEF, *FOOD & WINE* MAGAZINE

CAT CORA
CRAB AND AVOCADO "SANDWICHES" WITH MANGO COULIS

Nothing says warm-weather entertaining to me like these vibrant, tropical "sandwiches." I use very little breading in the cakes, which leaves room for lots of sweet lump crabmeat. When the crab combines with the fresh avocado salsa and smooth mango coulis, it makes for a delicious, bright, and beautiful dish.

SERVES 4 TO 6

2 cups canola oil

8 ounces Maine or Dungeness crabmeat

1 cup dry bread crumbs, plus more for breading

¼ cup mayonnaise or aioli

3 tablespoons finely chopped red onion

2 tablespoons thinly sliced scallions, white and tender green parts

2 tablespoons freshly squeezed lemon juice

1½ tablespoons finely diced red bell pepper

1½ tablespoons Worcestershire sauce

1 tablespoon Tabasco sauce

1 cup all-purpose flour

1 large egg, beaten

½ teaspoon salt

¼ teaspoon freshly ground black pepper

Mango Coulis (recipe follows)

Avocado Salsa (recipe follows)

Fresh cilantro leaves, for garnish

1. Heat 1 cup of the oil in a 10-inch sauté pan set over high heat. Reduce the heat to medium. Check the temperature of the oil with a thermometer. It should read 375°F.

2. While the oil is heating, combine the crabmeat, the 1 cup bread crumbs, and the mayonnaise, onion, scallions, lemon juice, bell pepper, Worcestershire sauce, and Tabasco in a medium mixing bowl. Mix until fully incorporated. Form four to six 3-ounce crab cakes.

3. Place the flour, egg, and extra bread crumbs in separate shallow bowls. Season the flour with the salt and pepper. Dredge the crab cakes in the flour, dip them into the beaten egg, and bread them lightly with bread crumbs. Lay the cakes in the hot oil and pan-fry for 5 to 6 minutes. Remove and place on a paper towel.

recipe continues

4. To serve the crab cakes, spoon some coulis onto each plate, forming a small pool. Slice a crab cake in half and lay the bottom portion in the coulis. Spoon some avocado salsa on top, and place the top of the cake on the salsa like a sandwich. Top with a small amount of salsa and garnish with a cilantro leaf.

AVOCADO SALSA

MAKES 3 CUPS

2 avocados, pitted, peeled, and cut into small dice

2 tablespoons freshly squeezed lime juice

2 tablespoons finely diced red onion

1 tablespoon minced fresh cilantro

1 tablespoon olive oil

¼ teaspoon salt

Combine the avocados, lime juice, onion, cilantro, oil, and salt in a medium mixing bowl. Mix well and refrigerate, covered, until ready to use.

MANGO COULIS

MAKE 4½ CUPS

2 mangos, peeled, pitted, and coarsely chopped

2 cups water

1 teaspoon confectioners' sugar

Combine the mangos, water, and confectioners' sugar in a blender and mix until smooth. Refrigerate, covered, until ready to use.

GUY FIERI
ALL-STAR SAUSAGE STEAK SANDWICH WITH GUID'S PICKLED HOT VEGGIES

The acid and sweetness of the veggies really rock the salt and heat of this sandwich. When you're doing a righteous sandwich like this, always use top-notch ingredients.

SERVES 6

2 pounds tri-tip

2 tablespoons Worcestershire sauce

1 tablespoon granulated garlic

1 tablespoon salt

1 tablespoon freshly cracked black pepper

2 tablespoons olive oil

1 pound Italian sausage links, hot preferred

2 cups thinly sliced yellow onions

2 cups julienned red bell peppers

3 tablespoons minced garlic

½ cup dry red wine

½ cup chicken stock

1 tablespoon hot paprika

1 tablespoon chili powder

1 teaspoon celery salt

1 large 18-inch-long sourdough loaf

¾ cup Guid's Pickled Hot Veggies (recipe follows)

6 slices provolone cheese

1. Heat a grill to high.

2. Rub the tri-tip with the Worcestershire sauce, granulated garlic, salt, and pepper. Let stand for 20 to 30 minutes.

3. Place the tri-tip on the grill and cook, turning it once, until medium-rare, 30 to 45 minutes. Set the meat aside to rest for at least 10 minutes.

4. In a medium sauté pan, heat the oil over medium-high heat; then add the sausage, onions, and bell peppers. Cook for 10 minutes, or until the onions are translucent. Add the minced garlic and cook for 2 minutes. Then deglaze the pan with the wine and stock. Lower the heat to a simmer and add the paprika, chili powder, and celery salt. Set aside.

5. Cut the loaf of bread in half lengthwise, remove some of the bread from the center, and toast the halves lightly under the broiler.

6. Slice the tri-tip as thinly as possible, on the diagonal.

recipe continues

7. Place the onion mixture on the bottom piece of bread. Slice the sausages into 6 slices per link. Add all the sausage slices to the onion mixture on the bread. Add the sliced tri-tip, and top with the Pickled Hot Veggies and the slices of cheese. Cover with the top of the loaf and cut into 2-inch-thick slices.

GUID'S PICKLED HOT VEGGIES

MAKES 3 CUPS

½ cup quartered garlic cloves

2 tablespoons plus ½ teaspoon salt

1 teaspoon black peppercorns

½ cup halved baby carrots

½ cup cauliflower florets

½ cup 1-inch pieces of celery

½ cup julienned Anaheim chile

¼ red bell pepper, julienned

¼ red onion, julienned

1¼ cups red wine vinegar

¼ cup extra-virgin olive oil

½ teaspoon red pepper flakes

½ teaspoon sugar

½ teaspoon freshly cracked black pepper

1 cup diced large Spanish olives

½ cup pitted and diced black ripe olives

¼ cup stemmed, seeded, and diced pepperoncini

1. Fill a large bowl with ice and water, and set it aside.

2. Bring a large pot of water (about 10 cups) to a boil. Add half the garlic, the 2 tablespoons salt, and the peppercorns. Blanch the vegetables, starting with the carrots: boil the carrots for 30 seconds. Then add the cauliflower and boil for 30 seconds; add the celery and boil 15 seconds; add the Anaheim chile, bell pepper, and onion, and boil for 15 seconds. Immediately remove all the vegetables from the water and submerge them in the ice bath. Discard the garlic and peppercorns.

3. In a large jar, place 1 cup of the vinegar, the oil, the remaining uncooked garlic, and the pepper flakes, sugar, cracked pepper, and remaining ½ teaspoon salt. Set aside.

4. Drain the cooled blanched vegetables and dice them. In a bowl, combine the olives, the pepperoncini, and the diced vegetables. Add the mixture to the jar containing the seasonings. Cap, and shake to mix. Top with the remaining ¼ cup vinegar to cover the vegetables, if necessary. Refrigerate for 24 hours. The pickled veggies will keep for 2 to 3 weeks under refrigeration.

"OKAY. LET ME GET THIS RIGHT: FOOD, WINE, SOUTH BEACH, AND I GET TO COOK. OH YEAH, I'M IN!"

—GUY FIERI

MICHEL NISCHAN
DRESSING ROOM MEAT LOAF

At my Westport, Connecticut, restaurant, Dressing Room, we're proud to serve meat loaf! Having this much-loved American standard on the menu is a comforting way for our guests to eat more sustainably by allowing us full use of the whole animal. Besides, who doesn't love a good meat loaf?

SERVES 6 TO 8

2 to 3 tablespoons olive oil

1 cup diced peeled parsnips
(2 to 4 parsnips)

¾ cup diced peeled carrots (about 2 carrots)

½ cup diced peeled celery root

⅓ cup diced onion

Kosher salt and freshly ground black pepper

2 cups soft fresh bread crumbs
(about 4 slices quality bread)

1 cup whole milk

2 large eggs, beaten

⅓ cup ketchup

3 pounds ground beef

1. Heat the oven to 375°F.

2. Heat the oil in a large sauté pan over medium-high heat. When it is hot, add the parsnips, carrots, celery root, and onion, along with a pinch of salt and pepper, and sauté for 6 to 8 minutes, or until softened. Set aside for 10 to 15 minutes to cool slightly.

3. In a large mixing bowl, mix together the bread crumbs, milk, eggs, ketchup, 1 tablespoon kosher salt, and ¼ teaspoon black pepper. Add the meat and cooked vegetables, and using a wooden spoon or your hands, mix well.

4. Transfer the meat mixture to a loaf pan, and bake for about 1½ hours, or until the meat loaf is cooked all the way through. An instant-read thermometer inserted into the center of the loaf should read 145°F.

5. Remove the pan from the oven, and serve the meat loaf straight from the pan. Slice it into serving pieces about 1-inch thick.

MARIO BATALI
ORECCHIETTE WITH SWEET SAUSAGE AND BROCCOLI

This is a classic dish from Puglia, one of my fave destinations and home to some of the most delish food in all of Italy. I chose this dish for SoBe in 2008 because it's simple to prepare for a large group. You can sub out the sausage with chopped salami, or delete the meat altogether and use a basic tomato sauce. You can also substitute any cruciferous or leafy vegetable for the broccoli . . . I love cauliflower or even escarole. You can make the pasta a week in advance and freeze it; just place the frozen shapes in a zip-lock bag and when you're ready to cook them, drop them straight into boiling water. We probably serve two dozen plates of this a night at Babbo, one of my New York restaurants. People really love the chewy texture of the noodle with the yin/yang of the sweet and fatty sausage and the astringent and vaguely bitter broccoli.

SERVES 6

5 tablespoons extra-virgin olive oil

1½ pounds pork sausage, ground

1 onion, cut into ½-inch dice

1 carrot, cut into ½-inch dice

½ rib celery, cut into ½-inch dice

1 cup red wine

½ cup crushed tomatoes and their juices

1½ pounds fresh orecchiette pasta (recipe follows) or good-quality dried pasta

Salt

4 cloves garlic, thinly sliced

1 teaspoon red pepper flakes

1 large head of broccoli, cut into 1-inch florets, nice stems sliced into ½-inch-thick slices

Freshly ground black pepper

Caciocavallo cheese, for grating

1. Heat 2 tablespoons of the oil in a large skillet or Dutch oven set over high heat. Place the sausage in the pan and allow it to cook, moving it occasionally to avoid sticking, until the fat has been rendered, 4 to 5 minutes. (You'll have to dump the rendered fat once or twice to avoid deep-frying the meat in its own fat.) Remove meat from pan and set aside.

2. Remove the excess fat from the pan, reduce the heat to low, and add the onion, carrot, and celery. Sweat the vegetables over low heat for about 6 minutes or until tender, letting them get soft but not browned. Add the red wine and scrape the bottom of the pan with a wooden spoon as you stir the wine in to dislodge the browned bits of meat. Add the

recipe continues

tomatoes, bring the mixture to a boil, and return the sausage to the pan. Reduce to a simmer and cook for 30 to 45 minutes, until the mixture is at ragù consistency, adding more liquid if necessary to keep the meat moist.

3. If you are making fresh orecchiette, prepare them while the ragù is cooking.

4. Bring 6 quarts of water to a boil and add 2 tablespoons salt.

5. While the water is heating, heat the remaining 3 tablespoons olive oil in a 12- to 14-inch sauté pan until almost smoking. Add the garlic, chili flakes, and broccoli and toss over high heat until the broccoli is tender, about 6 minutes. Add the ragù and toss over high heat for 2 minutes, seasoning it with salt and pepper.

6. Drop the orecchiette into the boiling water and cook until tender yet al dente, about 2 minutes (12 minutes for dried orecchiette). Drain the pasta and add it to the pan containing the broccoli and ragù. Toss over high heat for 1 minute. Divide evenly among 6 warm pasta bowls, grate caciocavallo over each bowl, and serve immediately.

ORECCHIETTE PASTA

4 cups semolina flour, plus more for dusting   1 to 1¼ cups tepid water

1. Place the flour in a large mixing bowl. Make a well in the center of the flour and add the water a little at a time, stirring well with your hands until the dough comes together. You may need more or less water, depending on the humidity of your kitchen.

2. Place the dough on a floured work surface, and knead it (like bread) for 8 to 10 minutes, or until smooth and elastic. Then cover it with a damp cloth and let it stand for 10 minutes at room temperature.

3. Cut the dough into 4 equal pieces and roll each one into a ¾-inch-thick cylinder (dowel). With a very sharp knife, cut small disks of ⅛-inch thickness from each cylinder. Press the center of each disk lightly with your thumb to form a saucer shape. Place the orecchiette on a sheet tray that has been sprinkled with semolina, cover with a clean dish towel and set aside.

"SOUTH BEACH IS PROBABLY THE BEST PLACE IN THE WHOLE COUNTRY TO PARTY AND COOK AT THE SAME TIME. I GET TO DO DEMOS WITH THE CRASHING WAVES AND THE BEAUTY OF THE BEACH AS A BACKDROP. AND THE TOWN IS JUMPING WITH REAL HOSPITALITY AND A GROOVY VIBE."

—MARIO BATALI

CLAIRE ROBINSON
SPINACH CARBONARA

I love a creamy pasta that's so perfectly satisfying I can skip the apps and dessert! This is my take on the classic, which epitomizes the beauty of few-ingredient cooking. The key to perfect carbonara is working while everything is piping hot; this ensures that the egg will cook and produce a silky, creamy sauce that sticks to the pasta.

SERVES 4

Salt

8 ounces slab bacon, cut into ½-inch chunks

1 pound fresh or dried spinach fettuccine

1 large egg plus 2 large egg yolks, at room temperature

1 cup grated Parmigiano-Reggiano cheese, plus more for garnish

2 teaspoons freshly cracked black pepper, or to taste

2 cups baby spinach leaves

1. Bring a large pot of water to a boil and salt it generously.

2. In a large high-sided skillet, cook the bacon over medium-high heat until crisp, about 10 minutes.

3. While the bacon cooks, drop the pasta into the boiling water and cook for about 4 minutes for fresh or according to the package instructions if using dried. When the bacon finishes crisping, remove the skillet from the heat.

4. Whisk the egg, yolks, 1 cup cheese, and pepper together in a small bowl. Set aside.

5. Return the bacon in the skillet to medium heat.

6. Using a ladle, slowly whisk about ½ cup of the pasta cooking water into the egg and cheese mixture until loosened.

7. Reserve some cooking water and drain the pasta; transfer the pasta to the skillet and toss until coated. While tossing continuously, slowly drizzle the egg mixture over the pasta until it's completely coated. Add more cooking water if the pasta seems dry. Add the spinach to the pan and toss until combined. Serve immediately, with cheese on top.

CHAPTER 6
MAIN
COURSES

If you're a foodie like I am, you know that the Big Question is not the meaning of life or nature versus nurture or the shape of the universe or any of that.

The big question is *What's for dinner?*

When people think of the SoBe fest, what first jumps to mind, I think, are walk-around tastings in huge tents or ballrooms: events such as the Burger Bash, the BubbleQ, the Best of the Best, and so forth. But we also host quite a few formal seated dinners and buffets along with all the casual parties.

These are the meals where the food takes center stage; where the venue, wine, and setting are all carefully chosen to showcase and highlight the work of a superlative chef or group of chefs. Over the years we've hosted more Michelin stars that we can count: Alain Ducasse, Michel Roux, Guy Savoy, Ferran Adrià, Elena Arzak, Eric Ripert, Daniel Boulud, Charlie Trotter, Thomas Keller, Jean-Georges Vongerichten, Nobu Matsuhisa, and Michael Mina are just a few of the superstars who have taken time from their super-busy lives to come down to the beach and cook.

I love the idea that some of the world's finest chefs will take their show on the road to help us raise money for a great cause. If a SoBe chef tells you that a festival weekend is just an excuse to party, don't even *think* of believing him. Our talent works every bit as hard here—harder, often—than in his or her own kitchen back home. They work with equipment they're not accustomed to, with ingredients from unknown purveyors, with help from cooks and sous-chefs they've never met.

Given all the issues at play, we're always a bit shocked, actually, at how magnificently our meals turn out. People frequently tell me that if SoBe were a restaurant, we'd get four-star reviews.

"I've been astonished by the quality of service and attention to details at the festival," says restaurateur Maguy Le Coze. "The banquet honoring Le Bernardin a few years ago attracted six hundred people and was perfection at every level: décor, service, and, of course, the delicious food prepared by our wonderful fellow chefs."

Chef Michael Mina agrees. "The food and wine at SoBe is absolutely top-notch," he says. "It's one of the many reasons that SoBe's one of the best events of the year.

Really inventive, talented chefs come and showcase their best work."

"As chefs, we love to be in such an exotic and sexy environment knowing that the quality of our food will not be compromised," says Le Bernardin chef/co-owner Eric Ripert.

Here are some of our favorite dishes—ones that are sure to wow your family or make a spectacular dinner party for friends.

GRILLED FOR ONE MINUTE
ROCCO DISPIRITO

Q: What's your favorite SoBe festival ritual? Do you have a regular restaurant, bar, or hangout?

A: I catch up with all my Miami friends and have a big dinner at Casa Tua, my favorite restaurant in Miami.

Q: What do you eat when no one is looking?

A: Hmmm. Let's just say it involves a pull tab and smells like canned sardines!

Q: What's the best advice you ever received?

A: Taste your food. It sounds fundamental, but you can't imagine how many chefs don't do it.

Q: If you could work with one chef, alive or dead, who would it be and why?

A: As a kid I always dreamed of working with Joël Robuchon. I used to live in the neighborhood in Paris where his restaurant Jamin was, and every day I passed it on my way to work. I stared into the room from the doorway and dreamed someday I'd learn how to make his famous potato puree.

Q: What has been the best day of your career so far?

A: When the *New York Times* three-star review of my restaurant Union Pacific was leaked to us.

Q: And the worst day?

A: It was just days after 9/11. Because our business, like others, was devastated, I had to lay off most of my staff at Union Pacific. These were cooks, waiters, hosts, and other wonderful employees who had been with us for a long time.

Q: If you could go up against anyone on *Iron Chef,* who would it be?

A: Anthony Bourdain and Gordon Ramsay.

OPPOSITE: (clockwise from top) Marc Ehrler (front row, without buttons) and the team in the kitchen at Loews Miami Beach in 2003. Alton Brown having a good time. Plating up for the festival tribute dinner.

ROCCO DISPIRITO

GRILLED CHICKEN CUTLETS WITH SAUTÉED BELGIAN ENDIVE, BACON, AND MANGO CHUTNEY

The first time I saw mango chutney used in a real kitchen was when I worked with Gray Kunz at Lespinasse in New York in 1993. It was one of about thirty ingredients used in a braised beef dish, and I thought, "This guy has cojones!" because he produced remarkable results by combining the most unlikely ingredients from random cultures. I like to think I was a good student, and I appreciate a great flavor combination when I see it. The bittersweet endive plus bacon plus mango chutney form an impressive alliance and elevate a simple grilled chicken cutlet to gastronomic greatness.

SERVES 4

4 chicken cutlets (about 1¼ pounds), pounded thin

2 tablespoons extra-virgin olive oil

Salt and freshly ground black pepper

8 ounces thick-cut bacon, cut into cubes

4 large Belgian endives, sliced crosswise about ½-inch thick

1 bunch scallions, white and tender green parts, sliced thinly on the diagonal

1 19-ounce jar Crosse & Blackwell Hot Mango Chutney

1. Heat a grill, grill pan, or broiler to high.

2. Coat the chicken with the oil and season with salt and pepper. Grill for 2 to 3 minutes per side, or until it is just cooked through.

3. Meanwhile, in a large sauté pan, cook the bacon over medium heat. When the bacon is golden brown, add the endive and scallions to the pan. Season with salt and pepper. Cook, stirring occasionally, for about 4 minutes, or until the endive is tender. Add the chutney to the pan and stir to combine. Season with salt and pepper, if necessary.

4. Serve the chicken cutlets topped with the bacon-endive-chutney mixture.

"WE'RE ALL HERE AT SOBE BECAUSE WE LOVE TO COOK AND EAT TOGETHER. YOU CAN EAT THE BEST MEAL IN THE WORLD ALONE, BUT HOW MUCH FUN WOULD THAT BE? THAT WOULD SUCK."

—ROCCO DISPIRITO

JEAN-GEORGES VONGERICHTEN
RACK OF LAMB WITH GREEN CHILE, MINT, AND SWEET PEA PUREE

This dish combines my favorite flavors and textures: sweet, spicy, crunchy. When I was creating it, I knew I wanted to throw in a hot chile punch. Lamb with mint is such a classic combination, but I added the mint to the lamb to cool the fire from the chiles. The sweet pea puree works as both a vegetable and a condiment, and is perfectly complemented by the mint. Of course, I couldn't leave the dish without adding some crunch, and to me, there's nothing better than a golden bread-crumb crust on a lamb chop. Every bite is exciting.

SERVES 8

4 racks of lamb, cut in half

Salt

Unsalted butter

Fresh mint sprigs

2 green Thai chiles, split

Shallot Puree (recipe follows)

Chile Crumbs (recipe follows)

1 cup green almonds, shelled and peeled

2 tablespoons canola oil

2 shallots, minced

2 cups sugar snap peas, blanched and split

Freshly ground black pepper

Fresh peppermint leaves, thinly sliced, for garnish

Mint–Sweet Pea Puree (recipe follows)

1. Heat the oven to 200°F.

2. Season the racks of lamb well with salt. Cover the bottom of a roasting pan with some butter, mint sprigs, and the chiles. Place the lamb, fat side down, in the pan and cook for 10 minutes on each side. Remove the lamb from the oven and let it rest.

3. Heat a large sauté pan to searing hot. Turn off the stove. Place the lamb, fat side down, in the pan for a minute, then turn it over.

4. Heat a broiler.

5. Spread the Shallot Puree liberally over the fat side of the lamb, and then coat it liberally in the Chile Crumbs. Brown quickly under the broiler, and then slice the meat in half.

6. Sauté the almonds in the oil until golden. Add the minced shallot and sauté briefly; then toss with the sugar snap peas. Season with salt and pepper, and finish with the sliced mint. Serve with the lamb and the Sweet Pea Puree.

recipe continues

SHALLOT PUREE

1⅓ cups ¼-inch-thick slices of shallots

½ cup extra-virgin olive oil

1⅓ teaspoons salt

1 cup plus 2¾ tablespoons blanched and squeezed fresh peppermint leaves

1. In a saucepan, combine the shallots, oil, and salt and cook, covered, over medium heat until the shallots are completely soft (no color).

2. Put in a blender, add the mint, and puree until completely smooth. Set aside.

CHILE CRUMBS

1½ ounces panko bread crumbs

2 tablespoon olive oil

¼ teaspoon salt

¼ teaspoon minced green Thai chile

Sauté the panko in the oil with the salt until golden. Mix in the chile and set aside.

SWEET PEA PUREE

1 pound frozen baby peas, defrosted and well drained

2 teaspoons chopped grilled jalapeño

1⅓ teaspoons salt

1¼ teaspoon sugar

2 tablespoons unsalted butter

1. Combine the peas, jalapeño, salt, and sugar in a blender, and puree until completely smooth. Do not add any water. The longer it purees, the more liquid will be released to facilitate the pureeing.

2. Warm the puree with a little butter in a saucepan, stirring it with a rubber spatula, before serving.

ALAIN DUCASSE
FOIE GRAS TAPIOCA RAVIOLI WITH SUNCHOKE EMULSION

I first created this dish for my New York restaurant; later my chef Tony Esnault prepared it at the Eric Ripert/Le Bernardin Tribute Dinner at South Beach in 2007. I like bridging culinary cultures, blending flavors rarely seen together. Here, a very French tradition, foie gras confit, meets the sunchoke, a tuber cultivated by Native Americans before the arrival of white settlers. The ravioli subtly shows my inclination for Mediterranean cuisine, just as the tapioca is a tribute to my childhood. Putting the essence of these elements together in a seemingly straightforward recipe is what I believe cooking is all about. Each flavor is clearly recognizable and they all blend together delicately.

SERVES 4

DOUGH

1 cup all-purpose flour, plus more for dusting

7 large egg yolks

1 teaspoon olive oil

Salt

RAVIOLI

1 quart chicken stock

1 cup small pearl tapioca

Salt

4 ounces foie gras confit

1 tablespoon butter

1 tablespoon minced fresh chervil

Salt and freshly ground black pepper

1 large egg, lightly beaten

GARNISH

1 lemon

8 ounces sunchokes

2 tablespoons butter

2 tablespoons olive oil

¼ cup chicken stock

1 clove garlic

1 sprig fresh thyme

Salt

2 stalks celery, peeled and cut into small dice

EMULSION

¾ cup whole milk

¾ cup chicken stock

2 tablespoons butter

1 clove garlic

1 sprig fresh thyme

GLAZE

½ cup plus 2 tablespoons chicken stock

2 tablespoons butter

FOR THE DOUGH

Place the flour in a mound on a smooth work area and create a well in the center. Add the egg yolks, oil, and salt to taste to the middle of the well. Slowly pull the flour into the eggs until incorporated. Finish kneading by hand, adding more flour if needed for a smooth consistency. Divide the pasta in half, and roll out each half on a lightly floured surface, or feed it through a pasta machine, until thin.

FOR THE RAVIOLI

1. In a saucepan, bring the stock, tapioca, and salt to taste to a boil. Cook until the tapioca is tender; then strain, and set it aside. Dice the foie gras confit and the butter, and allow to come to room temperature. Pass the confit and butter through a fine sieve, and mix with the tapioca and chervil. Season with salt and pepper.

2. To assemble the ravioli, flour a smooth work surface. Lay out the 2 sheets of pasta. Divide the filling into 24 equal portions and place 2 inches apart on one sheet of pasta. Brush the beaten egg over the pasta between the mounds of filling. Cover with the other sheet of pasta. Form ravioli by using the back of a 1-inch ring cutter to press the edges together; then cut out ravioli with a 1¼-inch ring cutter. Refrigerate or freeze until ready to use.

FOR THE GARNISH

1. Fill a medium bowl with water, and squeeze the lemon juice into it.

2. Peel the sunchokes, reserving the peelings, and cut them to the desired shapes. Submerge them in the acidulated water until ready to cook.

3. Heat the butter and 1 tablespoon of the oil in a saucepan over medium heat. Add the sunchokes, stock, garlic, thyme sprig, and salt to taste, and simmer until tender, about 4 minutes. Set aside.

4. In a small skillet, sauté the celery in the remaining 1 tablespoon oil, adding salt to taste. Cook until tender but still crunchy, 3 to 4 minutes. Chill the celery immediately.

FOR THE EMULSION

In a saucepan, combine the milk, stock, reserved sunchoke peelings, butter, garlic, and thyme sprig, and simmer for 30 minutes. Remove from the heat, strain, and set aside.

TO COOK THE RAVIOLI

In a pot of boiling salted water, cook the ravioli for approximately 2 minutes. Remove from the water, and set aside.

FOR THE GLAZE

Bring the stock and butter to a boil in a small saucepan. Cook, whisking constantly, until thickened to make a glaze. Brush the ravioli with glaze and season with salt and pepper.

TO FINISH

Brush the sunchokes with the glaze, and divide among 4 bowls. Top with ravioli and diced celery. Mix the emulsion with a hand blender to create foam, and spoon it around the ravioli.

TYLER FLORENCE
SLOW-ROASTED PORK SHOULDER WITH SALSA VERDE AND GRAINY-MUSTARD MASHED POTATOES

This recipe is one of my all-time favorites, as it shows how you can transform a relatively lean, tough cut of meat into something juicy and succulent that falls apart with the weight of a fork. The rub has toasted fennel seed in it, and when it combines with the roasted pork fat, the taste is out of this world. I serve the pork with a slather of raisin-caper salsa verde—the sweetness of the raisins and the saltiness of the capers add the perfect burst of bright flavor with every mouthwatering bite. And what better to serve it all with than delicious mustardy mashed potatoes?

SERVES 6 TO 8

2 tablespoons fennel seeds

¼ cup chopped fresh rosemary

¼ cup chopped fresh sage

4 cloves garlic

4 tablespoons kosher salt (1 tablespoon for every pound of meat)

1 tablespoon coarsely ground black pepper

¼ cup extra-virgin olive oil

1 boneless pork shoulder (about 4 pounds)

Salsa Verde (recipe follows)

Grainy-Mustard Mashed Potatoes (recipe follows)

1. In a small skillet set over medium heat, toast the fennel seeds until fragrant, about 2 minutes. Set aside.

2. Place the rosemary, sage, garlic, fennel seeds, salt, and pepper in a food processor, and pulse. Add the oil as it blends, to form a paste. Take the paste and rub it all over the pork. Cover the pork with plastic wrap and marinate in the refrigerator for at least 3 hours or up to overnight.

3. Allow the meat to sit at room temperature for 30 minutes before cooking.

4. Heat the oven to 325°F.

5. Place the pork, fat side up, in a roasting pan fitted with a rack. Roast the pork, loosely tented with aluminum foil, for 3 hours. Remove from the oven and let the meat rest on a cutting board for 15 minutes before slicing.

6. Serve with Salsa Verde and Grainy-Mustard Mashed Potatoes.

recipe continues

SALSA VERDE

½ cup golden raisins, soaked in warm water until plump

½ cup salt-packed capers, rinsed

4 cups roughly chopped fresh flat-leaf parsley

¼ cup finely chopped shallots

Juice of 2 lemons

1 teaspoon grated lemon zest

1 tablespoon Dijon mustard

Extra-virgin olive oil

Kosher salt and freshly ground black pepper

Drain the raisins. Roughly chop the raisins and capers. In a large mixing bowl, combine the parsley, raisins, capers, shallots, lemon juice, zest, and mustard. Add some oil to bring the mixture together. Season with salt and pepper. Refrigerate for 30 minutes to allow the flavors to come together before serving.

GRAINY-MUSTARD MASHED POTATOES

1 cup heavy cream

4 tablespoons unsalted butter

3 large Yukon Gold potatoes, peeled

1 teaspoon kosher salt

Freshly ground black pepper

¼ cup olive oil (optional)

3 tablespoons whole-grain mustard

1. In a small saucepan set over medium heat, warm the cream with the butter until the butter melts; set aside.

2. Put the potatoes in a medium saucepan, and cover with cold water. Bring to a boil; then add the salt. Reduce the heat and simmer for 15 to 20 minutes, or until the potatoes are very tender. Drain.

3. Pass the potatoes through a food mill or a ricer into a large mixing bowl. Stir in the warm cream mixture until it is absorbed and the mixture is smooth. Season with salt and pepper, and finish off by stirring in the oil, if desired, and the mustard.

GRILLED FOR ONE MINUTE
ALAIN DUCASSE

Q: What do you eat or drink when no one is watching?

A: An "energy shot" that my wife, Gwenaëlle, prepares for breakfast. It's an incredible mix of linseed, cereals, and raisins, with fresh fruits like kiwi and lemon. She also adds soy yogurt for the smoothness, and she boosts it with pollen and honey. Detox and energy effects guaranteed!

Q: Over the years, you've worked with many of the best chefs in the world. Who in particular did you love working with and why?

A: There are four. Before age twenty, I worked with Michel Guérard, a leading figure in nouvelle cuisine, and Gaston Lenôtre, who was redefining the art of pastry. My encounter in 1977 with Roger Vergé was also crucial, since he introduced me to Mediterranean cuisine. In the late '70s, I discovered Alain Chapel, whose style and personality left an indelible imprint on me.

Q: If you were to close all your restaurants tomorrow, what would you do next week? Next month? Next year?

A: Next week, I'd invite all my friends for a gigantic party in my house in the Basque country. Next month, I'd go to the remote places of the world where I don't yet know the cuisine. Next year, I'd open a restaurant.

Q: How is the America you now know different from what you expected?

A: Many years ago, when I first arrived in the U.S., I must confess I was polluted by the usual European prejudice about American food. Yet I did what I always do: get to know the country, its mind and mood, to invent a cuisine which fits with its psyche and habits. I traveled intensively and met the producers; I met a host of wonderful people, passionate about their products. That was an unexpected facet of the U.S.—and now I'm a fervent ambassador.

MICHAEL SCHWARTZ

HARISSA-SPICED BLACK GROUPER WITH ROASTED EGGPLANT, CHICKPEAS, AND ROASTED RED PEPPER VINAIGRETTE

Lusty and full of personality, this dish combines the just-cooked fish with a room-temperature "salad" of roasted eggplant mixed with raw shallots and herbs, creating a really nice contrast in textures and temperatures. With the exception of the fish, this dish can be prepared well in advance.

SERVES 6

4 tablespoons harissa paste

About 1¾ cups extra-virgin olive oil

2 tablespoons water

6 grouper fillets (6 to 8 ounces each)

4 pounds eggplant

Salt and freshly ground black pepper

1 15-ounce can cooked, drained chickpeas

6 shallots, thinly sliced

1 bunch fresh mint, roughly chopped

1 bunch fresh parsley, roughly chopped

Nonstick cooking spray

1 10-ounce jar roasted peppers, drained

½ cup sherry vinegar

Lettuce leaves, for garnish

1. Heat the oven to 450°F.

2. In a large nonreactive bowl, mix the harissa, 2 tablespoons of the oil, and the water. Add the fish and mix to coat the fish thoroughly. Cover and refrigerate until ready to use.

3. Rub the eggplant with 3 tablespoons olive oil, and season with salt and pepper. Place on a baking sheet and bake for 30 to 35 minutes, or until soft. Set aside until cool enough to handle. Then split the eggplant open with a knife and scoop the flesh away from the skin, discarding the skin. Roughly chop the eggplant. In a large bowl, combine the eggplant with the chickpeas, shallots, mint, parsley, and 6 tablespoons olive oil. Season with salt and pepper. Set aside at room temperature.

4. Spray a baking sheet with nonstick cooking spray. Place the fillets on the sheet, drizzle with some olive oil, season with salt and pepper, and bake for 10 to 12 minutes.

5. While the fish is cooking, place the roasted peppers, 1 cup olive oil, and the vinegar in a blender. Blend until it's the consistency of salad dressing. Season with salt and pepper.

6. Spoon the sauce onto 6 plates. Arrange the eggplant mixture on top. Place the fish on the plates, and garnish with lettuce. Serve and enjoy!

MARK MILLER
CINNAMON-BRINED LAMB LOIN WITH SOUTHWEST POLENTA AND SWEET MINT CORN

Among the delightful dishes I experienced as a student in Morocco were sweet/savory lamb tagines, where the lamb is cooked slowly in a dome-shaped earthenware covered pot that condenses the perfume of the saffron, ginger, garlic, and spices. At the end, you add sweet dates and ground cinnamon for more complexity. I've used this flavoring technique in many dishes, and this lamb, created for South Beach, was one of them.

SERVES 3 TO 4

8 cups cold water

¼ cup sugar

1½ tablespoons kosher salt

12 long Mexican cinnamon sticks (about 2 ounces), crushed

12 large cloves garlic, lightly smashed

2 tablespoons red pepper flakes

½ teaspoon liquid smoke

2 dried bay leaves

2 small drops cinnamon oil (optional)

1 teaspoon dried thyme leaves

4 whole star anise, roughly ground

2 tablespoons coriander seeds, toasted and roughly ground

1 tablespoon freshly ground black pepper

1 tablespoon fennel seeds, roughly ground

1 teaspoon cumin seeds, roughly ground

1 teaspoon allspice berries, roughly ground

2 large whole "frenched" racks of lamb (preferably Colorado lamb), cleaned (about 2¼ pounds, 7 ribs each, with very little fat cap left on)

Oil, for frying

Southwest Polenta (recipe follows)

Sweet Mint Corn (recipe follows)

1. In a deep stainless-steel or glass container, combine the water, sugar, and salt. Whisk to dissolve both. Add the cinnamon, garlic, red pepper flakes, liquid smoke, bay leaves, cinnamon oil (if using), and thyme. Then add the star anise, coriander, black pepper, fennel seeds, cumin, and allspice. (The ground spices should have the consistency of kosher salt.)

2. Place the lamb into the brine (the brine should cover the racks). Cover with plastic wrap and refrigerate for at least 24 hours or a maximum 48 hours (36 is optimal).

3. Drain the brine through a fine sieve into a bowl, and use this brining liquid to clean the racks of any spices that are adhering. (Do not wash under cold water as you will lose too much flavor.) Let the racks come to room temperature, about 2 hours.

4. Heat the oven to 450°F.

recipe continues

5. In a large ovenproof sauté pan, sear the racks in a little oil, without burning. Transfer the pan to the oven and roast for 6 to 8 minutes. The racks should register about 130°F in the center of the eye. Let them rest, and then cut into double chops, two ribs per chop.

6. Serve polenta on dinner plates, with two double chops on top and sweet corn on the side.

SOUTHWEST POLENTA

MAKES 6 CUPS

3 cups water

1 cup apple cider

1 cup Bob's Red Mill Corn Grits Polenta

½ cup dried Russian corn or other dried corn, ground into flour

1½ cups thinly sliced dried apples or apple bits (make your own overnight or use store-bought)

1 cup pine nuts, toasted

4 tablespoons butter, at room temperature

1½ teaspoons kosher salt

1. Combine the water and the cider in a heavy-bottomed 3-quart stainless-steel saucepan, and bring to a boil over high heat. As soon as it boils, reduce the heat to low and pour the polenta in all at once. Cook, stirring constantly, for 10 minutes to 15 minutes, adding small amounts of water if the polenta gets thick. It should fall off a spoon at this stage.

2. Whisk in the ground corn, and stir for 5 minutes. Add the apples and cook, stirring, for 5 minutes. Remove from the heat and add the pine nuts, butter, and salt. The polenta should be creamy and moist and not sticking. Keep covered and hot.

SWEET MINT CORN

MAKES 2½ CUPS

2 cups fresh corn kernels

¾ cup water

3 tablespoons finely diced Fresno chiles, other sweet-hot chile, or red bell peppers

2 tablespoons unsalted butter

2 tablespoons very thin julienne of fresh mint leaves

1 teaspoon finely chopped hot cinnamon hard candy (optional)

Place the corn and water in a sauté pan, cover, and cook over medium-low heat for 4 minutes. Add the chiles and butter, and sauté for a few minutes. Remove from the heat, and stir in the mint and candies, if desired.

CINDY HUTSON
BLUE MOUNTAIN COFFEE AND COCOA–ENCRUSTED PORK TENDERLOIN WITH CHIPOTLE-HONEY GLAZE AND CREAMY MANCHEGO POLENTA

I spent many years importing and selling Jamaican Blue Mountain coffee in the United States. It's considered the Dom Pérignon of all coffees. It has a fantastic aroma and flavor that mix wonderfully with cocoa powder and mesquite. Here, the combination of the spicy sweetness of the chipotle-honey glaze and the fat from the pork makes for a perfectly balanced dish.

SERVES 8

¼ cup unsweetened cocoa powder

¼ cup ground Jamaican Blue Mountain coffee beans

¼ cup mesquite dry seasoning

1 tablespoon kosher salt

½ teaspoon cayenne pepper

4 to 5 pounds pork tenderloin, silverskin removed

¼ cup canola oil

2 tablespoons salted butter

1 cup Chipotle-Honey Glaze (recipe follows)

Creamy Manchego Polenta (recipe follows)

1. Heat the oven to 350°F.

2. Place the cocoa, coffee, mesquite seasoning, salt, and cayenne in a zip-lock bag, and shake until well combined. Place some of the mixture on a plate and roll the tenderloin around in the rub until it is evenly covered. Slice the tenderloin into 3-ounce medallions (roughly 24 pieces).

3. Heat a large skillet over medium-high heat, and add the oil and butter. Sear the pork medallions on each side: about 3 minutes for medium-rare, 4 minutes for medium, 5 minutes for well done.

4. Remove the medallions and place them on a plate. Remove the excess oil from the skillet. Return the medallions to the skillet and ladle the Chipotle-Honey Glaze over them to coat.

5. Remove from the heat and serve with the Creamy Manchego Polenta.

recipe continues

CHIPOTLE-HONEY GLAZE

MAKES 1¼ CUPS

1 cup honey

2 canned chipotles in adobo, minced

¼ cup water

Combine the honey, chipotles, and water in a small saucepan, and bring to a boil. Reduce the heat and simmer for 4 minutes.

CREAMY MANCHEGO POLENTA

MAKES 4 CUPS

4 tablespoons salted butter

½ cup minced shallots

2 cloves garlic, minced

2 tablespoons fresh thyme leaves

3 cups chicken stock

1 cup high-quality fine or coarse-grain polenta

½ cup heavy cream

¾ cup grated Manchego cheese

Kosher salt and freshly ground black pepper

1. Melt the butter in a saucepan, add the shallots and garlic, and cook over medium-low heat until tender, 5 minutes. Add the thyme, and then pour in the stock. Raise the heat, and when the liquid is almost ready to boil, slowly add the polenta.

2. Cook over low heat, stirring constantly with a whisk, making sure there are no lumps. Add the cream immediately and continue to stir. When the polenta is almost done (follow the cooking instructions on the package), about 20 minutes, whisk in the cheese. Season with salt and pepper.

MASAHARU MORIMOTO
BRAISED BLACK COD

In Japanese restaurants in the United States, black cod is often marinated in sweet miso. But I wanted to introduce the SoBe audience to a black cod dish that's even more popular in Japanese homes as well as restaurants. Depending on the region and the season, this dish works well with almost any fish: try flounder, halibut, or even salmon. Basically, if you have sake, soy, sugar, and mirin, you can make it. I serve this in my restaurant and the fish becomes so soft and sweet that even kids love it.

SERVES 6

2 cups sake

6 slices fresh ginger

6 black cod fillets, skin on (6 to 7 ounces each)

1½ cups sugar

1 cup soy sauce

1½ teaspoons tamari soy sauce

3 tablespoons mirin

Scallions, white and tender green parts, julienned, for garnish

1. Pour the sake into a large, deep skillet. Add the ginger and the fish, skin side up. Cover, and cook over high heat for 3 minutes. Add the sugar and cook over medium-high heat for 3 minutes.

2. Pour the soy sauce and tamari over the fish. Continue to cook, covered, for 5 minutes. Add the mirin and cook for 3 minutes longer. Be careful not to burn the fish. Glaze the fillets by repeatedly pouring the thickened sauce over them while cooking.

3. With a slotted spatula, carefully transfer the fillets to a platter. Check the fish to make sure it has no residual bones hidden in it.

4. If the braising liquid is not thick enough, keep cooking it over high heat until it becomes caramelized.

5. Garnish the fish with the scallions and ginger, and drizzle with the braising liquid.

ALFRED PORTALE
"GRILLED" MAYAN SHRIMP WITH SPICED MANGO AND AVOCADO SALAD

I created this dish specifically for SoBe. We now serve it at Gotham Steak in the Fontainebleau Hotel (Miami Beach) and, in summer, at Gotham Bar & Grill in New York. The flavors are vibrant, spicy, and sexy, capturing the essence of South Beach.

SERVES 4

1½ pounds extra-large shrimp (3 to 4 per person), peeled and deveined

½ cup grapeseed oil, plus 2 tablespoons

3 cloves garlic, finely chopped

2 tablespoons smoked Spanish paprika

1 tablespoon finely grated orange zest

1 tablespoon coarsely cracked black pepper

¼ teaspoon plus a pinch of cayenne pepper

¼ cup freshly squeezed lime juice

1 generous teaspoon grated lime zest

1 teaspoon coarse salt

½ teaspoon Dijon mustard

¼ cup extra-virgin olive oil

Freshly ground white pepper

1 mango, peeled and cut into ½-inch dice

1 avocado, peeled and cut into ½-inch dice

½ small red onion, halved and thinly sliced (about ⅓ cup)

4 cups (loosely packed) soft lettuces, such as red oak-leaf or Lolla Rossa

1. Place the shrimp in a bowl. Prepare the marinade by pouring ¼ cup of the grapeseed oil into a small bowl. Add the garlic, paprika, orange zest, black pepper, and the ¼ teaspoon cayenne. Stir together. Set aside 1 tablespoon of the mixture, and pour the remaining marinade over the shrimp. Toss, cover, and refrigerate for at least 30 minutes and up to 6 hours.

2. Make the vinaigrette by whisking together the reserved tablespoon of marinade, the lime juice and zest, salt, mustard, and the remaining pinch of cayenne. Slowly whisk in the ¼ cup grapeseed oil, then the olive oil. Season with salt and white pepper.

3. Put the mango, avocado, onion, and lettuces in a large bowl. Dress lightly with ½ cup of the vinaigrette, or more if necessary, and season with salt and white pepper. Set aside.

4. In a sauté pan set over medium-high heat, heat 2 tablespoons grapeseed oil. Season the shrimp with salt and add them to the pan. Sear quickly, just over 1 minute on each side. Remove from the pan and cover to keep warm.

5. Mound the salad in the center of a platter and surround it with the shrimp. Serve family-style from the center of the table, passing any extra dressing alongside.

CHAPTER 7
DESSERTS

Desserts are anything but an afterthought at SoBe. Every year we invite some of the world's finest pastry chefs and bakers to come down and put the perfect finishing touches on our seated meals, dine-arounds, tented tastings, and all the other delicious events that make up the festival weekend.

To say we love sweets is the understatement of the century. You think *you* like to bake on the beach? Wait 'til you see how *we* do it.

Which is not to say that our desserts are all of the fancy, fine-dining persuasion. Over the years we've served cupcakes, Rice Krispy Treats, brownies, s'mores, chocolate chip cookies, marshmallows, strawberry short-cake, and ice cream galore. One year, in a packed amphitheater at Jungle Island, chef George Duran demoed chocolate soup for a standing-room-only crowd, then suggested dipping broccoli, carrots, and oranges into it to entice kids to eat their veggies. (It worked!) And I'll never forget the time that Alton Brown, at another kids' demo, used liquid nitrogen to make ice cream. I can still see the thrill on all those little faces, all these years later.

Sometimes the desserts are even the main event. Emeril's Sugar Shack, for example, was a late-night party held poolside at the Raleigh Hotel. Signature desserts from Emeril's restaurants were the raison

d'être, but the live music, crisp vintage Champagne, and fabulously retro water ballet show elevated the festivities from super to smashing. That night we served up 300 portions each of twelve different Emeril desserts, such as chocolate crêpes with espresso mascarpone, bourbon pecan tart with spiced crème fraîche, and chocolate–peanut butter cheesecake.

Then there was our Fifth Anniversary Party in 2006, our splashiest dessert extrava-ganza yet. Held poolside at the Loews Miami Beach, the party started at 10 p.m. after a gala dinner in honor of Ferran Adrià. Hedy Goldsmith led a baker's dozen of her fellow pâtissiers, each serving a different superstar dessert. The centerpiece was a huge and fittingly glamorous birthday cake flown in from New York on a private plane.

That was also the year we honored extraordinary baker and author Maida Heatter with a Lifetime Achievement Award. Maida is well into her eighties and has lived right here in Miami Beach, in the

SOBE SNAPSHOTS: HAVE GANACHE, WILL TRAVEL

WITH OUR FIFTH ANNIVERSARY COMING UP IN 2006, I KNEW WE WANTED A REALLY SPECIAL CAKE—SO I WENT TO SEE MARGARET BRAUN IN HER STUDIO IN NEW YORK'S WEST VILLAGE. SHE DOES THE MOST GORGEOUS CAKES, LIKE EDIBLE SCULPTURES.

"At the time I was working with lots of pinks and oranges, so Lee's timing was perfect," Margaret remembers. "I was like, *Yes! Tropical colors! South Beach!* Lee gave me total creative freedom."

The cake, designed to feed 500, would be the centerpiece of an event called Sweet Deco-Dence, held poolside at the Loews. We had invited thirteen top pastry chefs to prepare signature desserts, and Margaret's dazzling creation would be the star. We agreed on a dense chocolate blackout interior with a semisweet toffee crunch ganache, decorated exquisitely with sugar paste, *pastillage,* pearl dust, gold dust, and gold leaf. You know, just a simple little birthday cake. Margaret sent me a sketch and we were good to go.

Then it hit me: How the hell will we get this cake to Florida?

I turned to Terry Zarikian—as I often do—and next thing I knew, we had an invite to fly Margaret and the cake down from New York with Jeffrey Chodorow and his family and friends on their private plane. When Margaret got the news she was ecstatic: she says small jets are ideal for cakes because the luggage compartment, at the tail of the plane, is always chilly. I think she said something like "My cakes love to fly on private jets!"

Margaret remembers the flight as quite festive—"We ate pastrami sandwiches and laughed a lot"—but says she never really breathes easy until the plane lands and the cake is uncrated. "My mind is *always* on my masterpiece," she admits. "When I know a cake will travel, I use ganache. That makes it moist and fantastic, but also really strong. My traveling cakes are built to last . . . the SoBe cake could have survived the apocalypse."

Needless to say, the cake was breathtakingly beautiful and delectable. And before the first slice was ever cut, Margaret and I were already talking about what she would bake for our tenth anniversary!

same midcentury-modern house, for more than fifty years. In preparation for the award ceremony I visited her three or four times because she's just so much fun. Plus, she always gives you some fabulous cake, cookies, bonbons, or something else to take home. The Tribute meal was made by a remarkable team of chefs and served with wines from Domaines Barons de Rothschild (Lafite). Wolfgang Puck—so close to Maida that he's almost like a son to her—presented the award.

Pastry chef Jean-Marie Auboine and his team really took the cake for the elegant and over-the-top dessert buffet they created at SoBe in 2009. The event was the Best of the Best, the venue was the ballroom of the Fontainebleau Hotel (which had just reopened after its $500 million renovation), and the array of desserts (7,500 portions!)

was nothing short of spectacular: twenty different cakes and desserts, fifteen macaroons, ten flavors of marshmallow, sixteen handmade chocolates, six types of chocolate truffles, and so on. Jean-Marie has since moved on to become the executive pastry chef at Bellagio (Las Vegas), but that evening remains a standout. "My team was really happy to show what we could do," he remembers, "and the guests said *fantastique!*"

Even when it comes to something as simple as a favorite childhood sweet, we like to make a splash. To serve s'mores at the Burger Bash, we called candy queen Dylan Lauren—her Dylan's Candy Bar in Manhattan is the largest candy store in the world—and asked her to dream up the gooiest, yummiest, most creative s'mores that ever met a campfire. Then we dug fire pits on the beach, grilled skewers of marshmallows until golden, pressed them for appropriate ooze, drizzled with chocolate, dusted with nuts, and presented each one on a bed of colored sugar. It was all very Dylan-esque, and of course an absolute hit.

Desserts can be a bit challenging, of course, and sweets and heat don't always mix. In 2008, Claudia Fleming planned to serve coconut tapioca with passion fruit sorbet and basil syrup at a dinner honoring Jean-Georges Vongerichten. She made the coconut tapioca in her own restaurant kitchen on Long Island (her North Fork Table is one of our favorite restaurants of all time, by the way), then carefully packed it and shipped it via FedEx. Opening the boxes in Miami, she found that the containers had exploded, and she had to start all over in the Loews kitchen, the day before the event.

After all these years on the beach, we've figured out how to deal with just about any crisis: the fallen soufflés, the missing macaroons, the confiture confiscated at customs. Whatever it takes, our goal ten years on remains the same as it was that first year: to wow our guests and make sure they're happy when they head home. And one sure way to guarantee that seems to be to give them tantalizing desserts.

CLAUDE TROISGROS
CRÊPE PASSION

In Brazil, the passion fruit is incredible—my favorite fruit. I first created this dessert for a special dinner for Bill Clinton in Brasília and then began serving it in my restaurant. It's definitely a signature, and my customers love it. Passion fruit is available mostly in spring and early summer. When it's not, substitute any red fruit or pineapple.

SERVES 4

PASTRY CREAM

3 large egg yolks

⅓ cup sugar

1 tablespoon all-purpose flour

1 cup milk

1 vanilla bean, split and scraped

CRÊPES

10 large eggs, separated

1 cup sugar

1 cup plus 1 tablespoon all-purpose flour

2 cups milk

6 tablespoons butter, plus more for the pan

1 teaspoon baking soda

PASSION FRUIT SAUCE

8 ounces fresh passion fruit

¾ cup sugar

8 tablespoons water

2 tablespoons cold butter

Confectioners' sugar, for dusting

FOR THE PASTRY CREAM

1. In a mixing bowl, whisk the egg yolks with the sugar until light and fluffy. Add the flour.

2. In a saucepan, bring the milk, vanilla bean, and vanilla seeds to a boil. Remove the pan from the heat and gradually stir in the yolk mixture. Return the pan to the heat and bring to a boil, whisking constantly, and cook until thick, 1 to 2 minutes. Remove from the heat and let cool for at least 2 hours.

FOR THE CRÊPES

1. In a mixing bowl, whisk the egg yolks and ½ cup of the sugar until pale and smooth. Gradually add the flour.

2. In a saucepan, bring the milk and butter to a boil. Remove from the heat and let cool for 2 minutes. Then pour the hot milk into the egg yolk mixture, mixing well. Set the batter aside.

3. Heat the oven to 350°F.

recipe continues

4. In a clean bowl, beat the egg whites and the remaining ½ cup sugar until soft peaks form. Stir in the baking soda. Fold the egg white mixture into the batter.

5. Heat some butter in a 6-inch nonstick pan and add a generous ladle of the batter. Cook for 2 minutes on one side. Then remove the pan from the heat, place the crêpe on a baking sheet, and bake for at least 5 minutes. Repeat, making 3 more crêpes. When all the crêpes have been prepared, remove the baking sheet from the oven and let cool.

6. Fill each crêpe with a generous spoonful of the pastry cream. Then roll the crêpes closed, and set them aside.

FOR THE PASSION FRUIT SAUCE

1. Halve the passion fruits and scoop out the flesh and seeds into a medium bowl.

2. In a medium saucepan, combine the sugar and 1 tablespoon of the water. Cook on medium-high heat until the mixture turns a light caramel color. Remove from the heat. Add the passion fruit flesh, half of the seeds, and the remaining 7 tablespoons of water. Bring to a boil. Then lower the heat and simmer for 5 minutes. Stir in the butter until melted. Set aside.

TO FINISH

1. Dust the crêpes with confectioners' sugar. Caramelize the top of each with a blowtorch. Place the crêpes back in the hot oven, and cook until they get puffy and begin to soufflé, about 4 minutes.

2. Place each crêpe on a warm dessert plate, and top with the passion fruit sauce, sprinkle with the remaining seeds, and serve.

"AT SOBE THE ORGANIZATION IS IMPECCABLE, AND THERE ARE STAR CHEFS *EVERYWHERE*. IT'S A VERY NICE FUN WEEKEND WITH FRIENDS AND PEOPLE WE LOVE. IT'S REALLY AN INCREDIBLE EVENT."

—CLAUDE TROISGROS

GRILLED FOR ONE MINUTE
HEDY GOLDSMITH

Q: What was your earliest culinary influence?

A: My Easy-Bake Oven! Imagine the possibilities . . . baking with a sixty-watt lightbulb. Brilliant!

Q: Who inspired you early on?

A: Hands down, my earliest culinary influence was Julia Child. I sat motionless in front of our black-and-white TV, watching this larger-than-life superstar create magical dishes. She filled the screen with joy and passion.

Q: What is the most important thing you learned in culinary school?

A: At the Culinary Institute of America, I learned to quickly organize my ideas, size up a situation, and hit the ground running. Baking is like running a marathon, only better.

Q: At the Burger Bash in 2009, you served ice cream sandwiches of smoked bacon ice cream and buttered popcorn ice cream between smoked-sugar cookies. Is there a story behind that?

A: We do our own smoking at Michael's Genuine Food & Drink and it seemed like fun to apply a savory like bacon to dessert. They were like little sweet bacon sandwiches and nothing goes better with burgers than bacon! The popcorn ice cream is pure whimsy—we've served it in the restaurant. The crowd loved both of them.

Q: What is your most memorable SoBe moment to date?

A: Sitting next to Alice Waters, talking about our mutual culinary passions. Priceless! Thank you, Lee, for making that dream (and many more) come true.

HEDY GOLDSMITH
MILK CHOCOLATE CREMOSO WITH ESPRESSO PARFAIT

Sweet and salty, creamy and crunchy: if you close your eyes while eating a cremoso you may think it's the most delicious chocolate-covered pretzel. This dessert combines *all* the elements that make your senses sing. The perfect ending . . .

SERVES 10

CREMOSO

5 large egg yolks

2 cups heavy cream

⅓ cup granulated sugar

1 pound milk chocolate, coarsely chopped

ESPRESSO PARFAIT

2 cups heavy cream

½ cup confectioners' sugar

1 teaspoon vanilla extract

1 tablespoon brewed espresso, cooled

½ cup chopped hazelnuts

Extra-virgin olive oil

Sea salt

10 slices sourdough bread, toasted

FOR THE CREMOSO

1. Lightly whisk the egg yolks in a heatproof mixing bowl. In a saucepan, bring the cream and the sugar to a boil. Remove from the heat and slowly whisk into the egg yolks to temper them. Return the mixture to the saucepan and cook over low heat for 1 minute, or until thickened. Remove from the heat.

2. Place the chocolate in a heatproof bowl and pour the hot cream mixture over it. Whisk thoroughly. Spoon the cremoso into 10 small serving bowls or cups, cover them with plastic wrap, and refrigerate until the cremosos are completely firm, overnight or at least 8 hours.

FOR THE ESPRESSO PARFAIT

In a bowl, whisk the cream with the confectioners' sugar and vanilla until soft peaks form. Gently fold in the espresso, and spoon the parfait into 10 small ramekins. Freeze overnight or for at least 8 hours.

TO SERVE

Drizzle the cremosos with some oil and sprinkle with some salt. Top each with a garnish of hazelnuts. Place a ramekin of parfait to the side of each cremoso, and serve with the slices of toast.

RICK TRAMONTO
BRUSCHETTA OF LEMON RICOTTA AND BERRY MARMALADE kid friendly

I grew up in a traditional Italian family in Rochester, New York, and my grandmother, from Naples, lived with us. This was one of the treats that she'd make for breakfast. We had a family-style grocery in the neighborhood and it was easy to get Italian products, especially fresh ricotta. Make this on a Sunday morning with your kids or as a refreshing summertime dessert.

SERVES 4

1 cup ricotta cheese

Grated zest of 1 lemon, plus 1 tablespoon

Juice of ½ lemon

1 teaspoon freshly cracked black pepper

1 teaspoon kosher salt

¼ cup simple syrup (see page 30)

1 whole star anise

1 cup mixed strawberries, blueberries, and blackberries

8 ¾-inch-thick slices Italian bread

1. In a large bowl, combine the cheese, zest from 1 lemon, lemon juice, pepper, and salt. Mix until incorporated.

2. In a nonreactive saucepan, bring the syrup, star anise, and remaining 1 tablespoon zest to a boil. Reduce the heat and add the berries. Simmer until the berries have softened. Remove the star anise; discard. Remove the marmalade from the heat and let it cool. Set it aside.

3. Heat the oven on the broiler setting.

4. Place the bread on a baking sheet and toast under the broiler until golden brown on both sides. Remove from the oven. Spread each toast liberally with the ricotta mixture. Top each with a generous spoonful of the berry marmalade.

"ONE SOUTH BEACH MORNING, I GOT UP AT 7:30 A.M. TO GRAB A CUP OF COFFEE BEFORE I STARTED MY PREP, AND GOT ROPED INTO A LIVE RADIO PANEL ON THE BEACH WITH EMERIL, GAIL SIMMONS, AND MICHELLE BERNSTEIN. AND BEFORE I KNEW IT, WE ALL HAD GLASSES OF WINE IN OUR HANDS. ONLY IN SOUTH BEACH WOULD I BE DRINKING WINE AT 7:30 IN THE MORNING. ONLY WITH THESE FOLKS COULD THIS HAPPEN! WHAT A BLAST."

—RICK TRAMONTO

GINA AND PATRICK NEELY
WATERMELON SORBET

Gina says: I always love watermelon because it reminds me of sitting outside with my sisters. We weren't allowed to eat it in the house because it was so messy. We'd have a ball, spitting seeds at each other, not a care in the world. This sorbet is a great way to pay tribute to a favorite fruit. And because watermelon is so seasonal, it reminds me of a bright summer day. This recipe calls for minimum ingredients, and it's a pleasant surprise when you're hosting a party and want something light and pretty. If you add a little vodka to it, the party will just get better!

SERVES 4

1 cup sugar

½ cup light corn syrup

4 tablespoons freshly squeezed lemon juice

3 tablespoons grenadine

3 fresh mint leaves

1 3-pound seedless watermelon

1. In a small saucepan, bring the sugar, corn syrup, lemon juice, grenadine, and mint to a boil, cooking until the sugar dissolves. Remove from the heat and let cool slightly.

2. Cut off the rind of the watermelon, and cut the watermelon flesh into chunks. In a blender, puree half of the watermelon chunks. Strain through a fine-mesh strainer into a large bowl. Repeat with the remaining watermelon. Add the slightly cooled syrup mixture and mix well. Place in a 2-quart plastic container, cover, and freeze for 3 to 4 hours.

MALKA ESPINEL
DRUNKEN MOJITO RUM CAKE

My desserts are influenced by local flavors as well as Latin and Caribbean ingredients. This dessert is based on Jamaican rum cake and the mojito, South Florida's most popular drink. The cake is moist and flavorful, and the addition of mint, lime, and rum makes it unique. It's always one of our customer favorites!

SERVES 8

Unsalted butter, at room temperature, for the pans

6 large eggs

¾ cup sugar

6 tablespoons unsalted butter, melted

¾ cup all-purpose flour, plus more for the pans

½ teaspoon baking powder

¼ cup finely chopped fresh mint

Grated zest of 2 limes

Mojito Syrup (recipe follows)

Vanilla ice cream, for serving

Mixed fresh tropical fruit, for serving

1. Heat the oven to 350°F. Butter 8 individual Bundt pans or one 8-inch Bundt pan, and dust with flour. Set aside.

2. In the bowl of an electric mixer fitted with the whisk attachment, combine the eggs and sugar. Place the mixture in a double boiler and cook over simmering water, whisking constantly, until the eggs are warm but not too hot. Return the mixture to the bowl of the electric mixer, and whisk until about tripled in volume. Add a little of the egg mixture to the melted butter; mix well. Fold the butter mixture back into the egg mixture. Set aside.

3. In a mixing bowl, sift the flour and baking powder three times. Carefully fold the flour into the egg mixture. Add the mint and zest; mix well. Pour the batter into the prepared pan(s). Bake for 12 minutes for individual-size cakes, or 35 minutes for a large cake.

4. Remove the pan(s) from the oven, and let cool completely. Then unmold the cake(s) and soak with the Mojito Syrup. Serve with vanilla ice cream and fresh tropical fruit.

MOJITO SYRUP

MAKES 1¼ CUPS

1 cup sugar

1 cup water

Peel of 1 lime

½ cup fresh mint leaves

¼ cup white rum

1. In a small saucepan, bring the sugar, water, and lime peel to a boil. Remove from the heat and add the mint. Let stand for 30 minutes to infuse.

2. Remove the mint leaves and the lime peel, stir in the rum, and pour over the cake.

FRANÇOIS PAYARD
CHOCOLATE-COCONUT CAKE

This cake was a sincere mistake! I had planned to pair a chocolate ganache with a coconut macaroon biscuit. As I was making it, I realized I had added too much egg white and was running out of coconut. But I decided to spread it out on a sheet pan and bake it anyway. The result? A delicious and very sweet mistake indeed.

SERVES 6 TO 8

COCONUT SPONGE

Nonstick cooking spray

1½ cups sugar

4 large eggs

3⅔ cups unsweetened dried shredded coconut

GANACHE

10½ ounces bittersweet chocolate, chopped

3½ ounces milk chocolate, chopped

1⅔ cups heavy cream

GARNISH

1 cup unsweetened dried shredded coconut, toasted

FOR THE COCONUT SPONGE

1. Heat the oven to 350°F. Spray the bottom and sides of a 17½ x 12½-inch rimmed baking sheet with cooking spray and line it with parchment paper.

2. Fill a medium saucepan one-third full of water and bring it to a simmer. In the bowl of an electric mixer fitted with the whisk attachment, whisk the sugar and eggs until pale yellow. Place the bowl over the pan of simmering water and cook, whisking constantly, until the egg mixture is warm to the touch. Return the bowl to the mixer and beat the egg mixture on high speed for about 5 minutes, or until it has doubled in volume. Using a rubber spatula, fold in the coconut just until blended.

3. Pour the batter onto the prepared baking sheet, and using the rubber spatula, spread it evenly in the pan. Bake for 20 to 25 minutes, or until the top of the cake is light golden brown and a toothpick inserted in the center comes out clean.

4. Remove the baking sheet from the oven, place it on a wire rack, and let cool for 15 minutes.

recipe continues

5. Run a small sharp knife around the sides of the pan to loosen the cake. Place a wire rack over the cake and invert. Carefully peel off the parchment paper (the cake is extremely delicate). Cool the cake completely.

FOR THE GANACHE

Combine the bittersweet chocolate and the milk chocolate in a large heatproof bowl. In a medium saucepan, bring the cream to a boil. Immediately pour the hot cream over the chocolate. Whisk until the chocolate is completely melted and smooth. Cover the ganache with plastic wrap, pressing it directly against the surface, and refrigerate for about 4 hours, or until it is firm enough to spread.

TO ASSEMBLE THE CAKE

Trim off any uneven edges from the cake and cut it crosswise into three equal rectangles; each should measure about 5 by 10 inches. Place one of the rectangles on a serving platter. Using a small metal offset spatula, spread a generous layer of ganache over the top of the cake layer. Repeat with the remaining cake layers and ganache. Spread the remaining ganache over the sides of the cake. Sprinkle the toasted coconut over the top and sides. If not serving immediately, refrigerate the cake. (The cake can be made up to 1 day ahead. Bring to room temperature before serving.)

PAULA DEEN
DOUBLE CHOCOLATE GOOEY BUTTER CAKE

This is my signature dessert and my favorite variation on my Gooey Butter Cake recipe. Serve it with fresh whipped cream or softened vanilla ice cream.

SERVES 20 TO 24

1 18¼-ounce package chocolate cake mix

3 large eggs

1 cup (2 sticks) unsalted butter, melted, plus butter for greasing the pan

1 8-ounce package cream cheese, at room temperature

3 to 4 tablespoons unsweetened cocoa powder, to taste

1 16-ounce box confectioners' sugar

1 teaspoon vanilla extract

1 cup chopped unsalted nuts

1. Heat the oven to 350°F. Lightly butter a 13 x 9-inch baking pan.

2. In a large bowl, combine the cake mix, 1 egg, and ½ cup of the melted butter. Stir until well blended. Pat the mixture into the prepared pan and set it aside.

3. In the bowl of a stand mixer fitted with the paddle attachment, or using a hand mixer, beat the cream cheese until smooth. Add the remaining 2 eggs and the cocoa powder, and beat until well mixed. Reduce the speed to low and add the confectioners' sugar. Beat until well mixed. Slowly add the remaining ½ cup melted butter and the vanilla. Beat until smooth. Using a rubber spatula, stir in the nuts. Spread the filling over the cake batter in the pan.

4. Bake the cake for 40 to 50 minutes. Be careful not to overcook the cake: the center should still be a little gooey when finished baking. Remove the cake from the oven and let it partially cool on a wire rack before slicing and serving.

❝THE FESTIVAL IS ONE EVENT THAT FILLS ME WITH EXCITEMENT EVERY YEAR. THE SEXINESS OF TROPICAL SOUTH BEACH COMBINED WITH THE ALLURE OF THE EXCITING EVENTS MAKES THIS THE ULTIMATE CULINARY EXTRAVAGANZA!❞

—PAULA DEEN

NIGELLA LAWSON
CARAMEL CROISSANT PUDDING

This is what we Brits consider "pudding," which is far removed from its American incarnation. For this version, think bread pudding, only so much more luxurious: sweet, softly solid, and starchy, offering solace to the soul and bolstering the body. To eat it is heaven. When I make this for supper (most often on a Monday when I have staling croissants left over from the weekend), we eat nothing else. Why would one need to?

SERVES 2

2 stale croissants

½ cup sugar

2 tablespoons water

½ cup heavy cream

½ cup whole milk

2 tablespoons bourbon

2 large eggs, beaten

1. Heat the oven to 350°F.

2. Tear the croissants into pieces and place them in a small gratin dish. (I use a cast-iron oval one with a capacity of about 2 cups.)

3. Combine the sugar and water in a saucepan, and swirl around to help dissolve the sugar before placing the saucepan on the burner over medium to high heat.

4. Caramelize the mixture by letting it bubble away for 3 to 5 minutes, or until it turns a deep amber color. Keep looking but don't be too timid.

5. Reduce the heat to low and add the cream—ignoring all spluttering—and, whisking, the milk and bourbon. Any solid toffee that forms in the pan will dissolve easily if you keep whisking over low heat. Take the pan off the heat and, still whisking, add the beaten eggs. Pour the caramel-bourbon custard over the croissants, and if the croissants are very stale, let the pudding stand for 10 minutes to steep.

6. Bake the pudding for 20 minutes. Remove from the oven and prepare to swoon.

CLAUDIA FLEMING
SWEET CORN ICE CREAM WITH BLACKBERRY COMPOTE

One of the most highly anticipated crops on eastern Long Island is the Silver Queen corn. It's incredibly juicy and sweet and not at all starchy. It makes a crazy delicious ice cream that pairs perfectly with sweet, tart blackberries. The combination is the essence of summer here on the North Fork.

SERVES 8

4 ears sweet summer corn, preferably white	¾ cup sugar
3 cups milk	8 large egg yolks
1 cup heavy cream	Blackberry Compote (recipe follows)

1. Slice the kernels off the cobs, letting them fall into a large saucepot. Break the cobs into thirds and add them to the pot. Add the milk, cream, and half (6 tablespoons) of the sugar. Bring to a boil. Remove from the heat. Remove the cobs and set them aside. Using an immersion blender, puree the corn mixture in the pot. Return the cobs to the pot and let stand for 1 hour to infuse. Remove the cobs.

2. Fill a bowl with ice and cold water, and set it aside.

3. Return the pot to the heat and allow it to come to a scald. Turn off the heat. In a small bowl, whisk the egg yolks with the remaining 6 tablespoons sugar. Slowly add 1 cup of the corn mixture to the yolks, whisking constantly. Add the yolk mixture to the pot, whisking. Cook over medium-low heat, stirring continuously with a heatproof rubber spatula, until the mixture thickens and coats the back of a spoon, 3 to 5 minutes.

4. Strain the custard through a fine-mesh sieve into a bowl, pressing down on the solids; discard the solids. Cool in the ice bath. Remove from the bath, cover with plastic wrap, and refrigerate for at least 4 hours.

5. In an ice cream maker, process the custard according to the manufacturer's directions. Place in an airtight container, cover, and freeze until ready to serve in dessert bowls atop Blackberry Compote.

recipe continues

BLACKBERRY COMPOTE

4 cups fresh blackberries (4 ½-pint containers)

3 to 4 tablespoons sugar, to taste

Orange liqueur

1. In a small bowl, combine 1 cup of the blackberries with the sugar. Let stand for at least 15 minutes to macerate. Then puree in a blender, and strain through a fine-mesh sieve into a clean bowl; discard the solids.

2. Stir in the liqueur to taste. Add the remaining 3 cups berries, and toss to combine.

WINE WITH DESSERT: SOME PERFECT PAIRINGS

THE DESSERT COURSE IS OFTEN OVERLOOKED AS AN OPPORTUNITY FOR WINE PAIRING, SAYS ERIC HEMER, SOUTHERN WINE & SPIRITS' MASTER SOMMELIER. LESS-SWEET WINES WORK BEST WITH LESS-SWEET DESSERTS, WHILE RICH SWEET DESSERTS, LIKE A CHOCOLATE FUDGE CAKE, FOR EXAMPLE, PAIR BEST WITH RICH, FLAVORFUL, SWEET WINES, LIKE PORT. HERE ARE SOME OF ERIC'S FAVORITE MATCHES.

APPLE PIE AND LATE-HARVEST RIESLING. The green apple and crisp lime flavors of the wine work perfectly with this classic dessert. Semi-sweet Vouvray or California Chenin Blanc makes a good alternative.

BERRIES WITH LIGHTLY SWEET SPARKLING WINE. Fresh berries are lightly sweet and tart, requiring a wine with similar characteristics. Brachetto d'Acqui is a ruby red sparkling wine from Northern Italy with red fruit nuances that are perfect for fresh strawberries. Moscato d'Asti is also good.

CHOCOLATE CAKE WITH RUBY PORT OR BANYULS. Chocolate can overpower lighter dessert wines. Port and Banyuls are reds made from dark-skinned grapes with a lot of body and flavor, and both are "fortified wines" with a higher alcohol content, giving them extra body to stand up to the richness of a chocolate dessert.

CRÈME BRÛLÉE WITH SAUTERNES. Here's a match surely made in heaven: creamy-sweet caramel dessert meets wine with rich texture and sweet aromas/flavors of orange peel, honey, toffee, vanilla . . . mmm!

FRUIT SORBETS WITH SPARKLING MOSCATO. Here's the light-on-light version of dessert and wine. Moscato d'Asti is *frizzante,* or lightly sparkling, with a low (5.5 percent) alcohol content. It's fresh, light, grapey sweet, and terrific with sorbet.

VANILLA ICE CREAM WITH TAWNY PORT OR PX (PEDRO XIMENEZ) SHERRY. Forget the hot fudge or caramel sauce; try one of these dessert wines on top instead.

MICHAEL LAISKONIS
CHOCOLATE CASHEW TART

We produced several hundred of these tarts for the 2007 SoBe Tribute Dinner honoring my bosses at Le Bernardin, Eric Ripert and Maguy Le Coze. The dessert has since found a home on our menu in some form or other; my favorite variations include peanuts and hazelnuts. What makes this tart appealing—besides its taste and texture—is the fact that each component can be prepared a day or two in advance and then assembled at the last minute.

SERVES 8

2½ cups all-purpose flour, plus extra for dusting

1 cup almond flour

½ cup plus 1 tablespoon sugar

¼ cup unsweetened cocoa powder

½ teaspoon fine sea salt

¾ cup (1½ sticks) unsalted butter, at room temperature, cut into pieces

2 large egg yolks

2 tablespoons water

½ cup salted cashews, crushed

Caramel Filling (recipe follows)

Chocolate Ganache (recipe follows)

Candied lemon peel, chopped, for garnish

Ice cream, for serving

1. In the bowl of an electric mixer fitted with the paddle attachment, combine the all-purpose flour, almond flour, sugar, cocoa powder, and salt. Gradually add the butter with the motor running. Add the egg yolks and water, and mix until just incorporated.

2. Turn the dough out onto a lightly floured surface. Form it into a flat rectangle and wrap it tightly in plastic. Place the dough in the refrigerator and let it rest for at least 1 hour or up to 2 days.

3. Remove the dough from the refrigerator and place it on a lightly floured surface. Roll it out until ⅛ inch thick. Brush away any excess flour, and cut out eight 3½-inch rounds.

4. Line a baking sheet with parchment paper. Place eight 2-inch ring molds on the baking sheet, and top them with the dough rounds. Trim the top edge, and press the dough into the base of each ring to ensure there are no air pockets. Refrigerate for 30 minutes.

5. Heat the oven to 325°F with a rack in the middle position.

6. Bake the shells for 7 to 8 minutes. Rotate the baking sheet and continue to bake for an additional 7 to 8 minutes. Remove from the oven and let the shells cool completely; then unmold them.

7. Arrange the tart shells on a clean baking sheet and line the bottom of each shell with some cashews, to reach about halfway up the sides. Reserve additional cashews for garnishing.

recipe continues

"I REALLY LOOK FORWARD TO SEEING ALL THE OTHER CHEFS AT SOBE. THERE'S AN INSTANT CAMARADERIE AND MUTUAL RESPECT. ALL EGOS ARE CHECKED AT THE GATE AND EVERYONE HELPS EACH OTHER OUT. I TAKE AWAY SOMETHING GREAT FROM EACH FESTIVAL, WHETHER IT'S A NEW FRIEND OR ANOTHER CHEF'S 'SECRET' TECHNIQUE."

—MICHAEL LAISKONIS

8. Warm the caramel if necessary, and spoon just enough to cover the cashews into each shell. The shells at this stage should be only one-half to two-thirds full, allowing ample space for the ganache. Let the tarts stand for up to 30 minutes to let the caramel set slightly.

9. Warm the ganache if necessary, and fill the remaining space in each tart with the ganache. Let the tarts stand for 30 minutes to 1 hour, at room temperature, to let the ganache set.

10. To serve, place a finished tart on the center of each plate, and garnish with some cashews, some candied lemon peel, and a scoop of your favorite ice cream.

CARAMEL FILLING

MAKES 2 CUPS

1¼ cups sugar

½ cup water

1 tablespoon glucose syrup

½ teaspoon freshly squeezed lemon juice

¾ cup heavy cream

2 tablespoons unsalted butter

1. Combine the sugar, water, syrup, and lemon juice in a medium saucepan. Cover the saucepan and cook to a dark amber color, about 8 minutes.

2. Meanwhile, in another saucepan, heat the cream until warm.

3. Remove the caramelized sugar from the heat and deglaze the pan with the warmed cream. Return the caramel to low heat and cook until the sugar has completely dissolved.

4. Remove from the heat and whisk the butter into the caramel.

CHOCOLATE GANACHE

MAKES 2½ CUPS

1 cup heavy cream

2 tablespoons glucose syrup

10 ounces 55% to 61% chocolate couverture, chopped

2 tablespoons unsalted butter, at room temperature

1. In a small saucepan, bring the cream and syrup to a boil.

2. Meanwhile, place the chocolate in a large heatproof bowl.

3. Remove the cream mixture from the heat and gradually pour it over the chocolate, stirring to emulsify. Let the ganache cool to 95°F, and then stir in the butter.

PIERRE HERMÉ
PLAIN OR FANCY LIGURIAN LEMON CAKE

Moist, lemony, and dotted with raspberries, this simple round cake gets much of its depth of flavor from the unexpected addition of extra-virgin olive oil. While mild Ligurian olive oil is my choice, any fine-quality olive oil that's not too assertive will give you what you're looking for—a cake with a rich aroma, a light olive taste, and a soft texture. Serve it plain, just out of the pan, or fancy: spread with meringue, browned in the oven, and finished with fresh berries.

SERVES 10 TO 12

Unsalted butter, at room temperature, for the pan

1¾ cups all-purpose flour, plus more for the pan

1½ teaspoons baking powder

1 cup sugar

Finely chopped zest of 2 lemons

4 large eggs, at room temperature

3 tablespoons whole milk, at room temperature

⅔ cup mild extra-virgin olive oil

7 tablespoons unsalted butter, melted and still warm

1 tablespoon freshly squeezed lemon juice

2 cups (1 pint) fresh raspberries

Meringue (optional, recipe follows)

1. Heat the oven to 350°F with a rack in the center position. Butter a 10-inch round cake pan and dust it with flour, tapping out the excess. Set it aside.

2. Sift the flour and baking powder into a mixing bowl. Set it aside.

3. Place the sugar and lemon zest in the bowl of an electric mixer. Rub the ingredients together between your fingers until the sugar is moist, grainy, and very aromatic. Fit the bowl into the mixer fitted with the whisk attachment. Add the eggs and beat on medium-high speed for about 3 minutes, or until the mixture is pale and thick.

4. Reduce the speed to low and add the milk. Add the flour mixture, beating until just incorporated. Then add the oil, melted butter, and lemon juice, and beat until just incorporated.

5. Pour about one third of the batter into the prepared pan. There should be just enough to form a thin, even layer. Top with enough raspberries to cover the batter. Pour on the remaining batter, using a rubber spatula to gently spread it so that it runs between the berries and just covers them. You'll have a very thin top layer of batter.

6. Bake the cake for 30 to 33 minutes, or until it is golden and pulls away from the sides of the pan; a knife inserted into the center of the cake should come out clean.

recipe continues

7. Remove the cake from the oven and unmold it immediately onto a cooling rack. Invert the cake so it is right side up, and let it cool. Once cooled, the cake is ready to serve. Decorate with meringue and fresh berries, if desired.

MERINGUE

1 large egg white

¼ cup granulated sugar

Confectioners' sugar

Fresh raspberries or a mixture of raspberries, strawberries, and blueberries, for decorating (optional)

1. Heat the oven to 475°F with a rack in the center position.

2. Place the cooled cake on a parchment paper–lined baking sheet.

3. In an impeccably clean, dry mixing bowl, whisk the egg white until it holds soft peaks. Add the granulated sugar in a slow, steady stream and continue to beat until the mixture forms firm, glossy peaks. Immediately spread the meringue over the top of the cake, using a metal icing spatula or a spoon. Dust with confectioners' sugar. Bake the cake for 4 to 6 minutes, or until the meringue is lightly browned. (Alternatively, you can brown the meringue outside the oven, using a blowtorch.) Top the meringue with the berries, if using, and serve immediately.

Note: Undecorated, the cake can be wrapped in plastic and kept at room temperature for at least 4 days or frozen for up to a month. However, once the cake is topped with meringue, it should be stored in the refrigerator and eaten that day.

"THE SOUTH BEACH FESTIVAL HAS A WONDERFUL ATMOSPHERE OF CONVIVIALITY AND WAS AN EXTRAORDINARY SHARING EXPERIENCE. IT REALLY IS AN EVENT OF EXCEPTIONAL QUALITY!"

—PIERRE HERMÉ

GRILLED FOR ONE MINUTE
NIGELLA LAWSON

Q: What's the one cookbook (not your own) you use most often?

A: I am not sure that I "use" cookbooks exactly, though I'm certainly addicted to them. I love reading them, drooling over them, dreaming of what I might cook from them. There are three that always live in my kitchen: Mario Batali's *Molto Italiano,* Anna Del Conte's *Gastronomy of Italy,* and Stephanie Alexander's *Cook's Companion.*

Q: What sort of restaurant would you love to open, and where?

A: I have no desire to open a restaurant. I relish the fact that I'm just a home cook, someone who feeds family and friends and has no need to heed fashion or fad. But sometimes— usually when I'm on holiday and have had wine at lunch—I fantasize about opening some tearooms in a remote part of Italy, say on one of the Aeolian Islands. I see a café filled with cupcakes, Victoria sponges, juicy fruitcakes, summer and syrup puddings, and other glories from the British sweets trolley.

Q: What do you eat when no one is watching? Or what's your idea of late-night snacking bliss?

A: I don't feel ashamed of anything I eat or any way I eat it. I eat with relish, when I want and what I want. But sometimes I splurge, it's true, and a late-night quiet time in the kitchen with the day's newspaper, a baguette, and half a pound of deliquescing blue cheese can be just the thing. Or, at other times, a toasted bagel slathered with too much butter, or a wedge of devil's food cake, or maybe some leftover chicken from the fridge (with mayo and some mango chutney), or a cold roast potato sprinkled with Maldon salt.

Q: What is the best advice you ever received?

A: When you have company coming, never cook something you haven't cooked before. Do what my mother referred to as a "dry run" by trying the recipe out on family (or very old friends) first.

MATT LEE AND TED LEE
STRAWBERRY-BUTTERMILK ICE CREAM

This super-easy dessert marries delicious summer berries with one of our all-time favorite Southern ingredients, buttermilk, which gives the ice cream an appetizing, cheesecake-like tang. We love to serve it in bowls with shortbread cookies crumbled over the top.

SERVES 6

4 large egg yolks

½ cup sugar

1¾ cups heavy cream

1¼ cups buttermilk

8 ounces strawberries, trimmed and quartered (about 1½ cups)

¼ teaspoon kosher salt

1. In a medium bowl, beat the egg yolks lightly with a whisk. Then add ¼ cup of the sugar and continue to beat for about 1 minute, or until the mixture is smooth and milky lemon-yellow in color. Set it aside.

2. In a small saucepan set over medium-high heat, heat the cream and ¾ cup of the buttermilk, stirring, for 6 to 8 minutes, or until a candy thermometer reads 150°F and only the barest wisps of steam rise from the liquid's surface.

3. Meanwhile, in a food processor, puree the strawberries, the remaining ¼ cup sugar, and the salt to make a smooth electric-red puree (if you prefer a chunkier fruit texture in the ice cream, underprocess, leaving chunks of fruit the size you desire in the liquid). Reserve.

4. Pour the cream mixture in a thin stream into the bowl containing the egg mixture, whisking constantly until the liquids are completely incorporated. Add the remaining ½ cup buttermilk and the strawberry puree, and whisk to combine.

5. Place the custard in a 1-quart container and refrigerate for 4 hours or overnight, until the custard is very cold but not frozen.

6. Transfer the custard to an ice cream maker and churn according to the manufacturer's directions for 15 to 35 minutes, or until it is very thick and holds its shape. It should be the consistency of a very thick milk shake.

7. Place the ice cream in a container with a tightly fitting lid. If there is any space between the surface of the ice cream and the lid, pat a sheet of plastic wrap onto the surface of the ice cream. Cover the container and freeze until the ice cream has hardened, about 2 hours.

8. Fifteen minutes before serving, remove the ice cream from the freezer and remove the plastic wrap. Serve small scoops of ice cream in individual bowls.

JACQUES TORRES
CHOCOLATE CHIP COOKIES

When I first arrived in the United States, it took me a while to understand America's love for cookies. One day, after a long walk in Central Park, a friend offered me a warm cookie with a glass of cold milk, and it was magic! The combination of caramelized brown sugar, the flavor of sweet butter, and the deep chocolate taste made it a great taste experience. That memory led me to create my version of this American classic, and my signature chocolate chip cookie was born. We now sell thousands of these a year in our stores, offering them up freshly baked, warm and gooey.

MAKES FIFTEEN 5-INCH COOKIES OR THIRTY 1½-INCH COOKIES

1½ pounds unsalted butter, at room temperature

¾ cup plus 2 tablespoons granulated sugar

1 cup plus 2 tablespoons (packed) light brown sugar

2 large eggs

1½ cups plus 2 tablespoons pastry flour

1½ cups bread flour

½ tablespoon salt

1 teaspoon baking powder

1 teaspoon baking soda

½ tablespoon pure vanilla extract

1 pound Jacques Torres House Selection 60% chocolate or other semisweet or bittersweet chocolate, coarsely chopped

1. Heat the oven to 350°F. Line baking sheets with parchment paper or nonstick baking pads; set aside.

2. In the bowl of an electric mixer fitted with the paddle attachment, cream the butter and both sugars. Add the eggs, one at a time, mixing well after each addition. Reduce the speed to low and add the flours, salt, baking powder, baking soda, vanilla, and chocolate; mix until well combined.

3. Using a 4-ounce scoop for larger cookies or a 1¼-ounce scoop for smaller cookies, scoop the cookie dough onto the prepared baking sheets, spacing the scoops about 2 inches apart. Bake until lightly browned but still soft, about 20 minutes for larger cookies and about 15 minutes for smaller cookies.

4. Let the cookies cool slightly on the baking sheets before transferring them to a wire rack to cool completely.

THANK-YOUS

It was 2007 when food writer Julie Mautner, on assignment for *Food Arts* magazine, walked up to me at SoBe and said, "Lee, why don't we write a festival cookbook?"

"Why don't we?" was my reply.

Julie wrote a terrific proposal. I called my friend and longtime supporter of the festival Jon Rosen, my agent at William Morris Endeavor and asked if he could help. Jon sent it to a few of his favorite publishing houses. We were thrilled when Clarkson Potter made an offer.

Julie jumped right in, calling SoBe chefs for their festival stories and recipes. Some chefs patiently sent recipe after recipe until we found the one we agreed was pitch-perfect. There were seven rounds of spreadsheets to keep the various chapters organized and hundreds of e-mails back and forth, clarifying ingredients, techniques, portion sizes, side dishes, head-notes, and more. Then Julie spent a year sifting through our collective memories and wove them all together to tell the SoBe story. In the process we became great friends and Julie became a cherished part of the SoBe family.

Thank you to each and every chef who sent us a recipe, whether it made it into the book or not. So many tantalizing dishes, so little space!

Thank you to Michael and Elaina Moran for testing all our dishes in just under two weeks. It was an amazing feat of culinary derring-do or, as Elaina calls it, "a total food frenzy."

Thank you to Karen Klees Bidard, who whipped our recipes into shape, making sure they're all clean, clear, correct, and easy to use. Her expertise and dedication were invaluable.

And to Liesel Davis, for her recipe formatting and computer skills.

Quentin Bacon surpassed even our highest expectations with his heavenly food photography. Thanks also to Lauren Volo (Quentin's sous-photographer) for her energy and attention to detail—on location in South Beach and in the studio in New York.

Before Quentin could shoot our dishes, of course, they all had to be prepared. It was a joy to work with chef/food stylist Lori Powell and her assistants, Adeena Sussman and John Bjostad. Thank you also to prop stylist Natasha Louise King and her assistant, Ashley Renck.

The following people and companies generously provided ingredients, dishes, tableware, linens, and spirits for photography: ABC Carpet and Home, New York City; Michael Laiskonis, executive pastry chef, Le Bernardin, New York; Carol Wallack, chef/owner, Sola Restaurant, Chicago; Whole Foods; Mark Pastore, vice president, Pat LaFrieda Meats, New York City; Brett Dunne, Southern Wine & Spirits.

Thank you to Pam Krauss for green-lighting this book before she left Clarkson Potter, and to our talented, enthusiastic, and patient editor, Emily Takoudes, for showing us first-timers how it's done. Also at Clarkson Potter, thanks to Doris Cooper for her wise counsel and steady hand. And to our art director, Jane Treuhaft; senior designer Jennifer Davis; and designer Paul McKevitt, who blended all the ingredients so beautifully. To the capable and tech-savvy Peggy Paul, for her great advice and unfailing helpfulness. And publicity director Kate Tyler and our supremely well connected publicist, Kim Yorio, who knows the cookbook business inside out.

Thanks to Allison Herman, of Southern Wine & Spirits, for legal counsel. And to RJW Collective for branding assistance.

I'd like to thank my family: my mom and dad, Marlene and Ken Schrager, for raising us in a home filled with love, happiness, good times, and good food. It wasn't until I went out into the world that I realized how rare and precious that is. I hope they're one-tenth as proud of me as I am of them.

And finally, thank you a million times over to my wonderful partner, Ricardo Restrepo, who never complains about my nutty, peripatetic life and gives me a great reason to come home. He keeps me grounded and keeps my priorities straight. When we met, Ricardo ate only because he was hungry and rarely gave food much thought. Now he clips articles from food magazines, picks the restaurants he wants us to try, and calls himself a foodie. (I laughed out loud the first time I heard it.) Ricardo, you will always be my favorite dinner companion!

FESTIVAL THANK-YOUS

The festival is an enormous logistical undertaking that takes eighteen months of planning to pull off. The list of those who've supported and helped us over the years could fill a book in itself. But certain people deserve an especially supersized shout-out . . .

First and foremost, to Southern Wine & Spirits (SWS), for giving me the best job in the world. I had no idea how fortunate I was, back in 2000, to be hired as director of media and special events. SWS is a legend in the industry, and to be part of its most exciting chapter—one of enormous growth and philanthropy—has been exhilarating and rewarding. It's not a job, it's an adventure!

Thank you especially to my bosses Wayne Chaplin, Harvey Chaplin, and Mel Dick, the company's owners and partners, for having the good sense to hire me in the first place and for handing me the checkbook ten years ago and never grabbing it back.

Also at SWS: Richard Booth (for supporting me and the festival unequivocally), Eric Hemer, our master sommelier (who answers every question with a smile), Sandra Wauquier (who oversees our wine seminars), Tim Wagner (for valuable assistance on site at wine seminars), Susan Pessoa (for attention to detail and unparalleled proofreading skills), Zoraida Suarez (our supplier coordinator and all-around bundle of fun), and Natalia Limbert (Susan and Zoraida's trusty assistant).

Jimmy Mancbach, who passed away in 2007, ran our boutique fine-wine division at SWS Florida, and was so instrumental in our early years.

Michael Aller ("Mr. Miami Beach") opened all the right doors, convincing the mayor and commissioners to support us. In fact, thanks to everyone at the City of Miami Beach and the Greater Miami Convention and Visitors Bureau. At the Miami Beach Visitor and Convention Authority, special thanks to Elsie Sterling Howard, Grisette Roque, Melanie Muss, Steven Haas, and Jeff Lehman.

Thanks also to:

My friend Jennifer Rubell, who listened to me when I returned from Aspen that first year and said, "Lee, you have to do a festival like that here in Miami!"

New York event columnist Ted Kruckel, who came to the festival in year one and said, "You gotta get Dana Cowin from *Food & Wine* down here—she'll love this," and called her. *Food & Wine*—and their parent company, American Express Publishing— went on to be one of our most loyal partners; the festival would not be what it is without their nine years of support as Presenting Sponsor. Spearheaded by Chris Grdovic, they gave us early-on credibility and national recognition.

Jon Rosen, at William Morris Endeavor, who encouraged all his famous clients (some of the country's top culinary personalities) to get involved. Thank you, Jon, for everything you've done and continue to do for me, the festival, and this book.

Will Schwalbe, Ed Victor, and Dan Halpern, all legends in the literary world, who have been so supportive and have opened so many doors for me over the years.

Brooke Johnson and all the great people that I work with at Food Network: Sergei Kuharsky, Bob Tuschman, Carrie Welch, Lauren Mueller, Katie Ilch, Bruce Seidel, Susie Fogelson, Amanda Melnick, Allison Paige . . . and everyone on the sensational Food Network test kitchen team.

Marvin Shanken and the rest of the gang at M. Shanken Communications and *Wine Spectator*: Samantha Shanken Baker, Thomas Matthews, Gordon Mott, and Bruce Sanderson. They're our partner on all high-end wine events and their stamp of approval gives us enormous credibility.

Each and every one of our other sponsors, who give generously of product and money and ask for little in return (well, most of them, anyway).

Festival managing director Devin Padgett, who came to work with us in 2003. Devin is the event and logistics expert who oversees the Grand Tasting Village's exhibitors, demos, seminars, talent, and food. He produces the Aspen Food & Wine Classic and works closely with Jaie Laplante and me on the South Beach and New York festivals.

SBWFF event managers Kelly Murphy, Elaina Moran, Randy Fisher, Randi Freedman, Susan Kleinberg, and Heidi Ladell. I know a thing or two about special events . . . and their events are very, *very* special. I've known each one of these people for at least fifteen years; all are dear friends and they were among the first to join the SoBe team.

All the talented photographers who have helped us over the years: Michael Katz, Harold Doan, Red Eye Productions, Seth Browarnik, Dale Stine, Michael Upright, Mitchell Zachs, Peter Richardson, and Michael Marko.

Tara Gilani, our historian, who produces wonderful videos. Image consultant Bill Stahl, who helps us keep our looks. Josh Beers, the creative genius behind our website.

Carol Press, who handles travel arrangements for festival talent and guests, dealing patiently with last-minute changes and special requests. And Melanie Miller, our transportation coordinator, who gets them smoothly from place to place and is available 24/7.

Michelle Minyard and Milenko Samardzich, who run our hospitality suite and green rooms and always make our talent and sponsors feel welcome. And Susan Holtzman, our unyielding gatekeeper, who manages credential access.

At Books & Books in Miami Beach, owner Mitchell Kaplan, for helping me with so many introductions in the early days, and Cristina Nosti, our go-to person for all things SoBe.

The great faculty and staff at the School of Hospitality and Tourism Management at Florida International University, especially past president Modesto Maidique, president Mark Rosenberg, Dr. Joe West, interim dean Joan Remington, Marcos Perez, Cristina Mendoza, Sue Gladstone, Rafael Paz, Lee Dickson, Chip Cassidy, Mohammad Qureshi, Pete Garcia, and Alex Duque. Thanks also to the FIU Publications Department for creating and producing many of our printed materials since year one.

Special thanks to Michael Moran, the FIU lead chef-instructor who coordinates student festival culinary work and food prep for the BubbleQ. And of course to all the FIU students who toil behind the scenes and out front so our celebrity chefs can shine and our guests have a great time. You amaze me time and again.

Terry Zarikian, Patron Saint of All Things SoBe, was our "culinary and PR director" for years, but "festival codirector" more accurately conveys his role; we were virtually interchangeable in the early days. After the festival found its footing, Terry took a bit of a step back, but still jumps in to tackle any task tossed his way. Terry's energy and passion know no boundaries. And his intuition, sensitivity, and sage advice have saved me more times than I'll ever admit. Our morning walks are my therapy and my favorite part of the day. (Whenever we're struggling to solve a festival issue, Terry and I pause and pray to "St. Floorplana," the name we've given to one of the many Virgin Mary statues along our route.)

Jeffrey and Linda Chodorow of China Grill Management were our original festival angels. They took on the BubbleQ as a project, lavishing us with time, money, advice, prep space, chefs, and whatever else we needed.

And then there's the gang in the SBWFF office (aka "my kids"), the hardest-working, most capable, most creative people *ever*. They inspire and amuse me; they've got my back and I never forget it. May the day come that I can actually pay them what they're worth! Until then, a million thanks to Patrick Jong (creative guru, marketing genius, and photo editor nonpareil), Elizabeth Nuell (world's best assistant and talent liaison), Ashley Shapiro (ticket dominatrix and event manager extraordinaire), Jackie Eisen (our vendor liaison), Kimberley Mullings (operations manager, event planner, and superstar in training), Devonie Nicholas (media manager *magnifique*), Christian Fombrum (go-to guy for everything), Kristen Sofge (making all our sponsors' dreams come true), Jason Trautmann (who holds the purse strings), and Alexandra Givner (our book intern and newest member of the team).

Also in the SBWFF office, our associate director, Jaie Laplante. Jaie came to us from the film industry, and quickly and cleverly applied all his business savvy to the food-and-wine world. Today he oversees finance, liability, human resources, venue issues—all the day-to-day operation things.

And Lori Ann Cox, who helped us in every way to become what we are today.

And Kimberly Spence, who in the early years managed to do the festival work of three people, all while doing her "real" full-time job for me at Southern Wine & Spirits.

Agency 21, our hardworking sponsor and fulfillment company. They get the sponsors in and keep 'em happy.

We're fortunate to work with two amazing PR firms: Robin Insley and Associates (nationally) and Susan Brustman and Larry Carrino (locally). Thank you for shining the media spotlight on us when we want it and flipping it off when we don't!

A huge thank-you to Jonathan Tisch, chairman and CEO of Loews Hotels, one of our earliest and strongest supporters. With warmth and generosity, Jonathan threw open the doors to his beautiful hotels, giving new meaning to the word "hospitality."

To Marc Ehrler, former executive chef of the Loews Miami Beach for six years of festivals. Marc opened his heart and his kitchen to all our out-of-town chefs, did whatever was necessary to keep them all happy, put out a million fires, and staged some of the most elegant meals in our ten-year history.

And to the next Loews Miami Beach executive chef, Gordon Maybury, for jumping in to fill the clogs so quickly when Marc Ehrler left Miami. You didn't miss a beat, Gordon, and it couldn't have been easy. You're brilliant.

And to Charlie Hines, Debbie Castillo, Shawn Hauver, Michael Darst, Sarah Murov, and everyone else at the Loews Miami Beach, for making the hotel our home away from home.

And to the Fontainebleau Miami Beach hotel, for hosting one of our most-successful, most-scrumptious annual events, the Best of the Best.

Thank you to all the sommeliers, presenters, authors, and other leading lights who have contributed so much time and expertise.

And finally, a million thank-yous to all the phenomenal chefs who drop what they're doing year after year to come down and cook for a great cause. You guys are the steak and the sizzle, the bread and the butter. Your generosity, skill, and joie de vivre blow me away every year.

THE DREAM TEAM

Over ten years, SoBe has welcomed most of the world's very finest chefs, pastry chefs, bakers, sommeliers, wine-makers, and beverage experts . . . plus thousands of other industry insiders, aficionados, personalities, and leading lights. We've done our very best to list them all here. Thanks to everyone for ten dazzling and delicious years.

Paolo Abbona
Tony Abou-Ganim
Ferran Adrià
Dr. Arthur Agatston
Marilisa Allegrini
Greg Allen
Ted Allen
Michael Altman
Serafin Alvarado
Luis Amezaga
Sunny Anderson
José Andrés
Tim Andriola
Gary Andrus
Alessia Antinori
Piero Antinori
Michael Antonorsi
Becky App
Nate Appleman
Govind Armstrong
Jean Arnold
Arthur Artilis
Elena Arzak
Jon Ashton
Jean-Marie Auboine
Gregory Balogh
Xavier Barlier
Elizabeth Barlow
Paul Bartolotta
Aitor Basabe
Ted Baseler
Joe Bastianich

Lidia Bastianich
Mario Batali
Jeni Bauer
Eric Baugher
Marco Bax
Rick Bayless
Alvavo Beade
Sabin Beaskoetxea
Stephane Becht
Domonique Befve
Jennifer Behar
Zach Bell
Etti Ben-Zion
Keyvan Benham
Rose Levy Beranbaum
Brian Berman
Michelle Bernstein
John Besh
Bob Betz
Wolfgang Birk
Miguel Angel Bizcocho
Georges Blanck
Keith Blauschild
John Blazon
Michael Bloise
Michael Blum
Pio Boffa
Cecile Bonnefond
Rob Boone
Sandro Botegga
Luc Bouchard
Patrick Boucher

David Bouley
Daniel Boulud
Anthony Bourdain
Tom Parker Bowles
James Boyce
Lorraine Bracco
Jimmy Bradley
William Bradley
Sean Brasel
Margaret Braun
Ralph Brennan
Terrance Brennan
Sean Brock
Bruce Bromberg
Eric Bromberg
Alton Brown
Ed Brown
Jennifer Brown
Warren Brown
Jean-François Bruel
Cyril Brun
Thomas Buckley
David Bull
David Burke
Anne Burrell
Joel Butler
Alberto Cabrera
Kenny Callaghan
Joey Campanaro
Colin Campbell
Christopher Cannan
Don and Rhonda Carano

Viviana Carballo
Floyd Cardoz
Andrew Carmellini
Fabrizio Carro
Nicola Carro
Anthony Carron
Cesare Casella
Chip Cassidy
Emile Castillo
Federico Ceretto
David Chang
Victor Charcan
Richard Chen
Michael Chiarello
Jeffrey Chodorow
Zach Chodorow
Jim Clendenen
Mauro Colagreco
Mary Colhoun
Tom Colicchio
Tino Colla
Reginald Collier
Kenneth Collins
Scott Conant
Clay Conley
Thomas Connell
Adam Cooke
Neil Cooper
Francis Ford Coppola
Cat Cora
Hendrick Cornelissin
Geoffey Cousineau

Colin Cowie
Dana Cowin
Emmanuel Cruse
John Cuevas
Andrea Curto-Randazzo
Tim Cushman
Ariana Daguin
Michael d'Andrea
Gary Danko
Joe Davidson
Jeffrey M. Davies
Rob Davis
Bobby Deen
Jamie Deen
Paula Deen
Dale DeGroff
Bernard de Laage de Meux
Fredric Delaire
Giada De Laurentiis
Robert Del Grande
Jean-Philippe Delmas
Eric De Rothschild
Baroness Philippine
  de Rothschild
John DeLucie
Karen DeMasco
Laura DePasquale
Tony DeRienzo
Traci Des Jardin
Herve Deschamps
Jean Paul Desmaison
Rocco DiSpirito
John Doherty
Gildas d'Ollone
Vinny Dotolo
Richard Doucette
Tom Douglas
Laurent Drouhin
Veronique Drouhin-Boss
Dominique & Cindy Duby
Alain Ducasse
Marcel Ducasse
Margaret Duckhorn
Wylie Dufresne
Ron Duprat
George Duran
Daniel Eardley
Aitor Echezarraga
Robert Egert
Marc Ehrler
Jonathan Eismann
Angelo Elia

Aitor Elizegi
Gordon Elliott
Aitor Elola
Todd English
Tony Esnault
Mary Sue Ewing-Mulligan
Carlos D. Falcó
Elizabeth Falkner
Dean Fearing
Susan Feniger
Gabriel Fenton
Marco Ferraro
José Ferrer
Guy Fieri
Bobby Flay
Claudia Fleming
Tyler Florence
Jose Flores
Chad Ford
Jeremy Fox
Clark Fraiser
Ken Frank
Bethany Frankel
John Fraser
Neal Fraser
Keith Freiman
Maria Frumkin
Katsuva Fukushima
Mark Fuller
Bryan Fyler
Mark Gaier
Angelo Gaja
Alex Gambal
Bernard Ganter
Rick Garced
Jose Garces
Dani Garcia
Ruben Garcia
Randy Garutti
Jean-Marie Gautier
Michelle Gayer
Anthony Giglio
Michael Gilligan
Bobby "G" Gleason
Suzanne Goin
Duff Goldman
Hedy Goldsmith
Juan Gomez
Misha Gomez
Renaud Gonthier
Adrian Gonzales
Carmen Gonzalez

Jesús Gonzalez
Juliana Gonzalez
Benoit Gouez
Richard Graeter
Johnny Graham
Laurent Gras
John Gray
Gael Greene
Alex Guarnaschelli
Michel Guérard
Mireille Guiliano
Robbin Haas
Ilan Hall
Gabrielle Hamilton
Steve Hanson
Ryan Hardy
Darryl Harmon
JD Harris
Caroll Harrod
Jeff Haskell
Maida Heatter
Kerry Heffernan
Eric Hemer
Marilu Henner
Shaun Hergatt
Ursula Hermacinski
Pierre Hermé
Daniel Hernandez
Aron Hess
Mark Hewitt
Ethan Hilman
Ingrid Hoffmann
Roberto Holz
Eitenne Hugel
Todd Hulse
Arvin Humes
Daniel Humm
Dawn Hurlbert
Junnajet Hurrapan
Cindy Hutson
Hung Huynh
Robert Irvine
Stephan Iten
Johnny Iuzzini
Frédéric Jaboulet
Madhur Jaffrey
Adish Jain
Kurtis D. Jantz
Frank Jeannetti
Maggie Jimenez
Star Jones
Becky Jordan

John Jordan
Koji Kagawa
Paul Kahan
Stephen Kalt
Howard Kaplan
Elizabeth Karmel
Rob Kaufelt
Stephan Kauth
Douglas Keane
Hubert Keller
Thomas Keller
Bill Kim
Eric Klein
Roxanne Klein
Howie Kleinberg
Christopher Kostow
Brian Koziol
Gabriel Kreuther
Ellie Krieger
Oliver Krug
Gray Kunz
Greg La Follette
Francesco Lafranconi
Emeril Lagasse
Jim Lahey
Michael Laiskonis
Daniel Lajoux
Padma Lakshmi
Gary Lampner
Zane Lamprey
Agnes Laplanche
Alexandra Marnier
  Lapostolle
Aitor Larranaga
Mike Lata
Louis-Fabrice Latour
Dylan Lauren
Nigella Lawson
Edgar Leal
Maguy Le Coze
Olivier Lebret
Michael Ledwith
Joe R. Lee
Katie Lee
Matt Lee
Sandra Lee
Susur Lee
Ted Lee
Donald Lefton
Joseph Lenn
Kenny Li
David Lieberman

Paul Liebrandt
Chris Lilly
Jake Linzinmeir
Anita Lo
Michael Lomonaco
Dewey LoSasso
Willis Loughhead
Tim Love
Michael Luboff
Randy Luedders
Severine Luke
Pierre Lurton
Ken Lyon
Grant MacPherson
Larry Maguire
Barry Maiden
Francis Mallman
Jacqui Malouf
Lynn C. Mansel
Maria Manso
Stephanie March
Dan Marino
Nate Martin
Daisy Martinez
Alvaro Martinez Gundin
Russell Martoccio
Steve Martorano
Bob Masuczek
Nobu Matsuhisa
Tom Matthews
Dean Max
Brini Maxwell
Gordon Maybury
Jeff McBride
Jason McClain
Jack McDavid
Steve McDonagh
Connie McDonald
Brandon McGlamery
Julie McGowan
Robert McGrath
John McLean
Don McLemore
Henry Meer
Spike Mendelsohn
George Mendes
Ted Mendez
David Merfeld
Danny Meyer
Jospeh Micatrotto
Robert Mignola
Mark Militello

Mark Miller
Robin Miller
Terry Miller
Todd Mark Miller
Mary Sue Milliken
Mike Mills & Amy Mills
Michael Mina
Myron Mixon
Sean Mohammed
Michele Moline
Marc Mondavi
Marcia Mondavi
Peter Mondavi Jr.
Peter Mondavi Sr.
Robert Mondavi
Tim Mondavi
Franck Monnier
Rick Moonen
Jason Morale
Masaharu Morimoto
George Morrone
Gordon Mott
Christian Moueix
Willy Moya
Olivier Muller
Barbara Muller-Rundquist
Marc Murphy
Jean-Luc Naret
Joan Nathan
Gina Neely
Patrick Neely
Tony Neely
Vince Neil
Candace Nelson
Willie Nelson
Joe Ng
Tung Nguyen
Pascal Nibaudeau
John Nicely
Tim Nickey
Fortunato Nicotra
Drew Nieporent
Michel Nischan
Fred Noe
John Nordin
Sean O'Connell
Bradley Ogden
Willis Olazabalaga
    Legarreta
Mark Oldman
Jamie Oliver
John Olney

Steve Olson
Ken Oringer
Louis Ortega
Frank Ostini
Pascal Oudin
Josh Ozersky
Harald Pagan-Coss
Jordi Panisello
Damian Parker
Robert Parker
Tom Parlo
David Pasternack
Bhavesh Patel
Alex Patou
Cindy Pawlcyn
François Payard
David Pearson
Zak Pelaccio
Francois Peltereau-
    Villeneuve
Alberico Penati
Adam Perry Lang
Ted Peters
Armen Petrossian
Charles Phan
Virginia Phillip
Francesca Plantea
Davide Piana
Philippe Pinon
Don Pintabona
Steven Pipes
Christian Plotczyk
Nicole Plue
Marc Poidevin
Naomi Pomeroy
Paul Pontallier
Alfred Portale
Michael Psilakis
Wolfgang Puck
Davide Pugliese
Stephan Pyles
Steve Raichlen
Gordon Ramsay
Frank Randazzo
Marc Randazzo
Kent Rathbun
Kevin Rathbun
Rachael Ray
E. Michael Reidt
Donn Reisen (deceased)
Andrea Reusing
Michel Richard

Maximilian Riedel
Eric Ripert
Jamie Ritchie
Missy Robbins
Frederic Robert
Yvonne Roberts
Andrea Immer Robinson
Claire Robinson
Pedro Robles
David Rodriguez
Douglas Rodriguez
Al Roker
Mitchell Rosenthal
Steven Rosenthal
Andrew Marc Rothchild
Benjamin Rottkamp
Michel Roux
Frederic Rouzaud
Oscar Rubin
Michael Ruhlman
Phillipe Ruiz
Michael Sabin
Arun Sampanthavivat
Bill Samuels
Marcus Samuelsson
Aaron Sanchez
Bruce Sanderson
Richard Sandoval
Andrea Santiago
Max Santiago
Miguel Santiago
Roberto Santibanez
Suvir Saran
John Sarich
Edmondo Sarti
Oliver Saucy
Carey Savona
Guy Savoy
Ed Sbragia
John Scharfenberger
Michael Schlow
Christian Schmidt
Richard Schnieders
Ian Schrager
Michael Schwartz
Mindy Segal
Christopher Sepe
Julian Serrano
Vita Shanley
Mark Shelby
Joe Shirley
Jon Shook

...Silverton
...o Silvestri
Gail Simmons
Kerry Simon
Alpana Singh
Art Smith
Dan Smith
John Sola
Tony Soter
Renato Spanu
Susan Spicer
Joachim Splichal
John Stage
Susie Stallings
Cal Stamenov
Jeffrey Starr
Jeffrey Steelman
George Stella
Sandra Stephani
Martha Stewart
Simon Stojanovik
Curtis Stone
Larry Stone
Alex Stratta
Tomas Strulovic
Pedro Subijana
Nori Sugie
Marc Summers
Allen Susser
Andrew Swersky
Michael Symon
Guillermo Tellez
John Tesar
Christian Thompson
Gabe Thompson
Francisco Torreblanca
Edfrank Torres
Jacques Torres
Miguel Torres
Laurent Tourondel
Fabio Trabocchi
Rick Tramonto
Loren Trefethen
Jean Trimbach
Claude Troisgros
Charlie Trotter
Ming Tsai
Michael Tusk
Monroe Udell

Albert Uster
Thomas Valenti
Marcela Valladolid
Jordi Valles
Norman Van Aken
Jon Vandegrift
Jacques VanStadem
Gary Vaynerchuk
Peter Vauthy
Freddy Vega
John Vergos
Marc Vetri
Johnny Vinczencz
Bryan Voltaggio
Michael Voltaggio
Baroness Andrea
    Von Simmern
Jean-Georges Vongerichten
Chuck Wagner
Yuji Wakiya
Tetsuya Wakuda
Carol Wallack
David Walzog
Chris Ward
Lisa Warren
Regynald Washington
Alice Waters
Jonathan Waxman
Vicki Wells
Laura Werlin
Kris Wessel
Josh Wesson
Jeff Weubsteub
Jasper White
Michael White
James Wierzelewski
Craig Williams
Marvin Woods
Jonathan Wright
Roy Yamaguchi
Martin Yan
Alan Yau
Sang Yoon
Gregory Yu
Matt Zagorski
Geoffrey Zakarian
Terry Zarikian
Mark Zeitouni
Sue Zemanick
Paul Zenga
Kevin Zraly
Bill Zuppas

RECIPE CREDITS

Ferran Adrià's Carrot Air with Bitter Coconut Milk: *El Bulli 2003–2004* (Ecco, 2006).

Michelle Bernstein's Smoked Ham and Cheese Croquetas: Adapted from *Cuisine à Latina: Fresh Tastes and a World of Flavors from Michy's Miami Kitchen* (Harcourt, 2008).

Daniel Boulud's Melon Salad with Lemongrass Shrimp: *Daniel's Dish: Entertaining at Home with a Four-Star Chef* (Filipacchi, 2003).

Tom Colicchio's Caramelized Tomato Tarts: *Think Like a Chef* (Clarkson Potter, 2007).

Cat Cora's Crab and Avocado "Sandwiches" with Mango Coulis: *Cat Cora's Kitchen* (Chronicle, 2004).

Paula Deen's Double Chocolate Gooey Butter Cake: *Paula Deen's Kitchen Classics: The Lady & Sons Savannah Country Cookbook* and *The Lady & Sons, Too!* (Random House, 2005).

Rocco DiSpirito's Grilled Chicken Cutlets with Sautéed Belgium Endive, Bacon, and Mango Chutney: *Rocco Gets Real: Cook at Home Every Day* (Wiley, 2008).

Alain Ducasse's Foie Gras Tapioca Ravioli with Sunchoke Emulsion: *Grand Livre de Cuisine d'Alain Ducasse* (Les Editions Alain Ducasse, 2007).

George Duran's Granny Smith Guacamole: *Take This Dish and Twist It* (Meredith Books, 2008).

Claudia Fleming's Sweet Corn Ice Cream with Blackberry Compote: *The Last Course: The Desserts of Gramercy Tavern* (Random House, 2001).

Tyler Florence's Slow-Roasted Pork Shoulder with Salsa Verde and Grainy-Mustard Mashed Potatoes: *Tyler Florence: Stirring the Pot* (Wiley, 2008).

Pierre Hermé's Plain or Fancy Ligurian Lemon Cake: *Desserts by Pierre Hermé* (Little, Brown, 1998).

Ingrid Hoffmann's Frozen Pops: *Simply Delicioso* (Clarkson Potter, 2008).

Katie Lee's Logan County Hamburgers: *The Comfort Table* (Simon Spotlight Entertainment, 2007).

Elizabeth A. Karmel's Texas Hill Country Brisket: Adapted from *Taming the Flame* (Wiley, 2005).

Emeril Lagasse's Sambal Shrimp Recipe courtesy of Emeril Lagasse, courtesy of Martha Stewart Living Omnimedia, Inc.; previously published in *Emeril at the Grill: A Cookbook for All Seasons* (HarperStudio, 2009.)

Padma Lakshmi's Sautéed Sweet Potato and Edamame: *Tangy Tart Hot and Sweet: A World of Recipes for Every Day* (Weinstein Books, 2007).

Nigella Lawson's Caramel Croissant Pudding: *Nigella Express: Good Food, Fast* (Hyperion, 2007).

Sandra Lee's Lemon-Cucumber Cocktail: *Semi-Homemade* magazine.

Chris Lilly's Bubble Q Pulled Pork: Adapted from *Big Bob Gibson's BBQ Book: Recipes and Secrets from a Legendary Barbecue Joint* (Clarkson Potter, 2009).

Nobu Matsuhisa and Thomas Buckley's Black Cod in Butter Lettuce Wraps: *Nobu Miami: The Party Cookbook* (Kodansha International, 2008).

Spike Mendelsohn's Colletti's Smokehouse Burger and Toasted Marshmallow Shake: *The Good Stuff Cookbook: Burgers, Fries, Shakes, Wedges, and More* (Wiley, 2010).

Masaharu Morimoto's Braised Black Cod: *Morimoto: The New Art of Japanese Cooking* (DK Publishing, 2007).

Jamie Oliver's Roasted Carrots and Beets with the Juiciest Pork Chops: *Jamie at Home: Cook Your Way to the Good Life* (Hyperion, 2008).

Michael Schlow's Schlow Burger with Cousin Shari's Coleslaw: *It's About Time: Great Recipes for Everyday Life* (Steelforth Press, 2005).

Martha Stewart's Lobster Roll: *Martha Stewart's Cooking School: Lessons and Recipes for the Home Cook* (Clarkson Potter, 2008).

Laurent Tourondel's BLT Grilled Tuna Sandwich: *Bistro Laurent Tourondel: New American Bistro Cooking* (Wiley, 2001).

Norman Van Aken's Chilean Seafood Pastel: *New World Kitchen: Latin American and Caribbean Cuisine* (Ecco, 2003).

"EACH TIME ONE OF OUR CHEFS IS INVITED TO COOK AT THE FESTIVAL, I CROSS MYSELF IN HOPES THAT THEY'LL ACTUALLY FEEL LIKE RETURNING TO WORK UP HERE IN NEW YORK."

—DANNY MEYER, RESTAURATEUR, UNION SQUARE HOSPITALITY GROUP

ABOVE: (left to right) Bobby Flay lovin' the crowd in 2009—and vice versa. Tom Colicchio was BubbleQ Host Chef in 2009. Masaharu Morimoto's Pork "Kakuni" Burger won "Best Dressed Burger" at the Burger Bash in 2010.

INDEX